PM Crash Course™
for IT Professionals

PM Crash Course™
for IT Professionals

Real-World Project Management
Tools and Techniques for IT Initiatives

Rita Mulcahy

Contributing Author: Martha L.Young

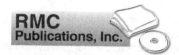

RMC
Publications, Inc.

RMC Publications
10953 Bren Road East
Minnetonka, MN 55343 USA

Cisco Press

Cisco Press
800 East 96th Street
Indianapolis, IN 46240 USA

PM Crash Course™ for IT Professionals

Rita Mulcahy and Martha Young
Copyright© 2010 Cisco Systems, Inc. and RMC Publications, Inc.

Published by:
RMC Publications, Inc.
10953 Bren Road East
Minnetonka, MN 55343 USA

Cisco Press
800 East 96th Street
Indianapolis, IN 46240 USA

Printed in the United States of America

First Printing   October, 2009

ISBN-13: 978-1-58720-259-9
ISBN-10: 1-58720-259-X
Library of Congress Cataloging-in-Publication Data available upon request.

Warning and Disclaimer

This book is designed to provide information about IT project management. Every effort has been made to make this book as complete and as accurate as possible, but no warranty of fitness is implied.

The information is provided on an "as is" basis. The authors, RMC Publications, Inc., RMC Project Management, Inc., Cisco Press, and Cisco Systems, Inc. shall have neither liability nor responsibility to any person or entity with respect to any loss or damages arising from the information contained in this book or from the use of the discs or programs that may accompany it.

The opinions expressed in this book belong to the authors and are not necessarily those of RMC Project Management, Inc., or Cisco Systems, Inc.

Trademark Acknowledgments

All terms mentioned in this book that are known to be trademarks or service marks have been appropriately capitalized. RMC Publications, Inc., RMC Project Management, Inc., Cisco Press, or Cisco Systems, Inc., cannot attest to the accuracy of this information. Use of a term in this book should not be regarded as affecting the validity of any trademark or service mark.

"PMP" and "PMI" are marks of the Project Management Institute.

Corporate and Government Sales

Corporations and Government agencies (Local, State and Federal) may receive special discounts on this book when orders are placed in quantities greater than five (5) copies. For more information on these special discount programs inside and outside of the United States, please contact RMC Project Management at (952) 846-4484 or via e-mail at info@rmcproject.com.

Feedback Information

At RMC Publications and Cisco Press, our goal is to create in-depth technical books of the highest quality and value. Each book is crafted with care and precision, undergoing rigorous development that involves the unique expertise of members from the professional technical community.

Readers' feedback is a natural continuation of this process. If you have any comments regarding how we could improve the quality of this book, or otherwise alter it to better suit your needs, you can contact us through e-mail at feedback@ciscopress.com. Please make sure to include the book title and ISBN in your message.

We greatly appreciate your assistance.

Americas Headquarters
Cisco Systems, Inc.
San Jose, CA

Asia Pacific Headquarters
Cisco Systems (USA) Pte. Ltd.
Singapore

Europe Headquarters
Cisco Systems International BV
Amsterdam, The Netherlands

Cisco has more than 200 offices worldwide. Addresses, phone numbers, and fax numbers are listed on the Cisco Website at **www.cisco.com/go/offices.**

CCDE, CCENT, Cisco Eos, Cisco HealthPresence, the Cisco logo, Cisco Lumin, Cisco Nexus, Cisco StadiumVision, Cisco TelePresence, Cisco WebEx, DCE, and Welcome to the Human Network are trademarks; Changing the Way We Work, Live, Play, and Learn and Cisco Store are service marks; and Access Registrar, Aironet, AsyncOS, Bringing the Meeting To You, Catalyst, CCDA, CCDP, CCIE, CCIP, CCNA, CCNP, CCSP, CCVP, Cisco, the Cisco Certified Internetwork Expert logo, Cisco IOS, Cisco Press, Cisco Systems, Cisco Systems Capital, the Cisco Systems logo, Cisco Unity, Collaboration Without Limitation, EtherFast, EtherSwitch, Event Center, Fast Step, Follow Me Browsing, FormShare, GigaDrive, HomeLink, Internet Quotient, IOS, iPhone, iQuick Study, IronPort, the IronPort logo, LightStream, Linksys, MediaTone, MeetingPlace, MeetingPlace Chime Sound, MGX, Networkers, Networking Academy, Network Registrar, PCNow, PIX, PowerPanels, ProConnect, ScriptShare, SenderBase, SMARTnet, Spectrum Expert, StackWise, The Fastest Way to Increase Your Internet Quotient, TransPath, WebEx, and the WebEx logo are registered trademarks of Cisco Systems, Inc. and/or its affiliates in the United States and certain other countries.

All other trademarks mentioned in this document or website are the property of their respective owners. The use of the word partner does not imply a partnership relationship between Cisco and any other company. (0812R)

About the Author

Rita Mulcahy, founder and CEO of RMC Project Management, is the most popular project management author in the world. Since 1991, hundreds of thousands of project managers have utilized her 30+ best-selling books and resources to expand their project management knowledge and further their careers. Rita speaks to thousands of executives and project managers each year, and has a reputation for helping people to learn and to have fun while doing it.

About the Contributing Author

Martha L. Young is president and founder of Nova Amber, LLC, a virtual business consultancy specializing in business process virtualization strategies and methodologies. She has co-authored three books and written dozens of articles and papers on the business value of virtualization. She has been engaged in the technology industry for nearly 20 years.

About the Technical Reviewers

Kelly Dwight holds a master's degree in Technology Management and a Certificate in Project-based Management from the University of Denver, is a practicing Project Management Professional (PMP)® with the Project Management Institute, and currently leads the USA IT Project Office for North America's largest natural gas producer. Ms. Dwight's career spans over fifteen years of project leadership experience delivering strategic business value in the areas of marketing, operations, and product management. She has overseen multi-million dollar programs, managed solutions life cycles from concept to sunset, and directed global portfolios introducing new products and services, in both private and leading Fortune 500 firms within Cable, IT, Oil & Gas, Retail, Software, and Telecommunications.

Blaise Stephanus, MS, PMP is an adjunct faculty member at the University of Denver and Information and Communications Technology Project (Cost Schedule) Manager on a $50,000,000 National Science Foundation Project in Boulder, Colorado. Blaise has had over 20 years of experience in the IT industry. He has held such positions as Senior Analyst, Systems Analyst, and Senior Project Manager. He also holds affiliations with Project Management Institute and IEEE. He holds a master's degree from the University of Colorado and a BS degree from Northeastern University.

Table of Contents

	Introduction	xi
Chapter 1:	Before You Read This Book	1
Chapter 2:	How to Use This Book	5
Chapter 3:	Understanding the Project Management Process	9
Chapter 4:	The Project Charter	27
Chapter 5:	Incrementalization: Breaking the Work into Projects	43
Chapter 6:	Gaining, Creating, and Using Historical Data	55
Chapter 7:	Identifying and Managing Stakeholders	65
Chapter 8:	Finalizing Project Objectives: The Project Scope Statement	87
Chapter 9:	Preventing Scope Creep: The Work Breakdown Structure and WBS Dictionary	99
Chapter 10:	Real-World Estimating	117
Chapter 11:	Real-World Scheduling	129
Chapter 12:	Communications Management	145
Chapter 13:	Preventing Problems: Identifying and Managing Risk	163
Chapter 14:	Saving the Failed or Failing IT Project	175
Chapter 15:	Measuring Success Post-Project	183
Chapter 16:	Next Steps	191
Appendix A:	Business Process Improvement Standards	195
Appendix B:	Project Management Software Considerations	199
Appendix C:	Real-World IT Interviews	203
Index		247

Introduction

Every part of every business depends on information technology. Consider the infrastructure behind a company's communication system. Does it support a rich feature set including working from a smart phone? The conferencing, forwarding, and follow features are all enabled through IT.

Consider the marketing communications department. This team often uses a wide variety of applications from bridge conferencing to video development and uploading. The marketing communications team needs desktop applications, publishing applications, Web development tools, video development and editing tools, and Internet search capabilities. All of these applications and tools are dependent on the IT infrastructure.

Just think of the amount of IT infrastructure behind the accounting department. This group doesn't function in isolation, their tools need to integrate with sales, shipping and receiving, and expense management. They have to be able to close the company's books in a matter of days at the end of each quarter and each year. The annual report the company produces each year has a list of tools a mile long that support its development.

When implemented correctly, IT can add significant value to the business. Technology and how it is used to grow a company can be, and often is, a competitive advantage. A business can attribute a rise in productivity, in large part, to technology and its ability to improve business processes. IT professionals are often faced with extremely challenging project deployments, as well as initiatives that are mission-critical to their organizations.

For IT project managers, a strong understanding of the discipline of project management is invaluable—both to success with individual projects and to their overall careers. However, while you have an idea of what project management is, are your perceptions accurate? Do you know that project management is a science and an art? Do you fully understand the difference good project management can make on your projects? Do you realize that there are key things you should do and not do?

By completely thinking through and mapping IT projects using project management methodologies and best practices, a project manager saves the project time and money, and increases the probability of project success.

The fact that you are reading this book indicates you realize that better knowledge of the discipline of project management will make a difference in how your projects have been going and how your own career in project management is progressing.

PM Crash Course™ for IT Professionals is full of project management tools that you can apply immediately to your IT projects—to deliver them on time, on budget, and with fewer headaches.

Scope of This Book

Please note, this book does not cover all aspects of project management. The scope of this book is to show you the tricks of where to focus your project management efforts to make the greatest immediate impact. The book will help you start controlling your projects rather than allowing them to control you. The end result of reading this book will be projects that are completed faster, cheaper, and easier. And of course, your reputation as a project manager will benefit immensely as well.

This is a business book with an emphasis on the value of integrating project management and technology in organizations. Focusing on project management creates high value productivity. It promotes a thorough and systematic process that emphasizes rapid identification, assessment, and response to the issues arising out of today's complex IT projects and environments.

By reading the book, completing the exercises, and answering the Questions for Discussion at the end of each chapter, you will gain a solid set of skills to immediately apply the discipline of project management, the methodology, and numerous best practice ideas.

Who Should Read This Book?

PM Crash Course™ for IT Professionals is intended for IT professionals like you, who find themselves responsible for completing a project, but who do not have formal project management training. You are looking for easy-to-use tools and processes to make an immediate impact on your current IT project. We believe this book distills the most important things you need to know in order to make a difference on your project right now.

How This Book Is Organized

This book is designed to be read quickly and easily cover-to-cover, beginning with an overview of IT project management and an all-important "How to Use This Book" chapter. It is also useful as a desk reference to keep handy throughout a project life cycle.

This revolutionary Course in a Book® covers the basics of project management, including planning, scheduling, budgeting, and more. It also moves beyond the basics to cover a number of real-world project management tools and techniques for IT initiatives—like defining IT project charters and requirements, breaking down IT roadmaps into manageable pieces, capturing and using historical data, identifying and managing stakeholders, defining IT project scope, and more.

The authors provide indispensable practical checklists, templates, and exercises to reinforce your learning of these concepts. The book includes dozens of tricks, insights, and contributions from real project managers sharing what has made a difference for them when managing real-world projects.

- **Chapter 1, "Before You Read This Book"**—This chapter serves as an introduction to the world of IT project management.

- **Chapter 2, "How to Use This Book"**—This chapter explains the numerous features within each chapter to make your learning more fun, interesting, and relevant to the real world.

The core chapters 3-15 cover the following topics:

- **Chapter 3, "Understanding the Project Management Process"**—This chapter identifies and defines the project management processes and the project life cycle, and the dynamic role of a project management plan. The chapter discusses how to identify key project constraints and explains how IT-centric processes complement project management methodologies.

- **Chapter 4 , "The Project Charter"**—This chapter defines the project charter and discusses the measurable metrics used to determine the success of a project.

Chapter 5, "Incrementalization: Breaking the Work into Projects"— Key concepts in this chapter include understanding the definition of a project, and identifying the differences between project, program, and portfolio management. It illustrates the value of breaking work into projects that can be planned, managed, and controlled.

Chapter 6, "Gaining, Creating, and Using Historical Data"—In this chapter you will learn the value of using historical information from past projects to take advantage of successes and avoid repeating the mistakes of others. You will also identify what type of project data is most beneficial to capture for the benefit of future projects. The practice of documenting historical information helps to continuously improve project process efficiencies.

Chapter 7, "Identifying and Managing Stakeholders"—Understanding who the stakeholders are on your project as well as what and how to communicate with them keeps everyone focused and is key to preventing problems throughout the project.

Chapter 8, "Finalizing Project Objectives—The Project Scope Statement"—This chapter outlines the difference between product and project scope and explains the business value of the project scope statement.

Chapter 9, "Preventing Scope Creep: The Work Breakdown Structure and WBS Dictionary"—This chapter is all about the hierarchical way to break a project into smaller, more manageable components or work packages as a major precursor to budgeting, scheduling, communicating, allocating responsibility, and controlling the project.

Chapter 10, "Real-World Estimating"—In this chapter, you identify the challenges in accurately estimating time or cost, and learn numerous techniques to improve estimating.

Chapter 11, "Real-World Scheduling"—This chapter describes how to create a realistic project schedule and teaches you how to read and understand a project management network diagram so you can define the critical path and use it to adjust the project to meet the required delivery date.

Chapter 12, "Communications Management"—This chapter describes how and why to develop an effective project communications management plan. It also covers the best ways to communicate specific types of information.

Chapter 13,"Preventing Problems: Identifying and Managing Risk"— This chapter defines risk management and explains the sequential and iterative process of risk management to increase opportunities as well as decrease threats.

Chapter 14, "Saving the Failed or Failing IT Project"—This chapter identifies the characteristics of a failing project and shows you the steps to take to save a failing project or to revive a failed project.

Chapter 15, "Measuring Success Post-Project"—In this chapter you learn how to measure the effectiveness and business impact of the project, and to understand the value end-of-project reports might provide across multiple departments in a company.

And the book ends with:

Chapter 16, "Next Steps"—In this chapter you are provided with a survey tool for assessing your project management skills. This chapter also provides encouragement and suggestions on how to improve your IT project management expertise and effectiveness.

The following appendices include additional information on topics introduced in the main text.

Appendix A, Business Process Improvement Standards—This appendix provides a high-level discussion of Six Sigma and ITIL.

Appendix B, Project Management Software Considerations—This appendix presents a list of features to consider when choosing project management software.

Appendix C, Real-World IT Interviews—In this appendix, you will find reflections from representatives of various-sized organizations regarding their experiences with the application of project management in the real world.

Did you know there are secrets to success in project management for IT? No matter how long you have worked on projects, or how much you already know, there are more secrets for you to discover. Many project managers have spent years self-teaching project management, only to discover with a challenging project that they do not actually know what they need to know to successfully execute the project. They learn, too late, some secret that would have made all the difference in the success of the project.

This book is designed to teach you the things you absolutely must know to successfully manage IT projects in the real world.

Look around you at work. Most people rarely get a chance to make a difference. Projects, on the other hand, are designed to make a change, make a difference, and make things better within your environment. Time spent learning more about the project management profession can help you increase the difference you are able to make, whether you work in IT or any other part of the company.

Before you continue reading, it might be time for you to make a decision. Simply reading this book is not enough. You have to decide to make changes in how you manage IT projects. IT projects are different from any other type of project in the company.

Information technology is a business enabler, playing an increasingly critical role in the success of a business. Networked technologies, from the Internet to collaboration technologies and telepresence, are becoming more intelligent and widely available today. Businesses of all sizes and markets are aligning more and more applications and processes with products and services. All these communication and business processes flow through an IT infrastructure. It is therefore even more essential for IT initiatives to execute, maintain, and evolve the interoperability of these systems. While IT is still considered either a cost of goods sold or operational expense, IT initiatives are now very much mapped to business goals and objectives and must be planned accordingly to ensure those goals are met.

Project management tools and methodologies will enable you and your team to not only understand but to quantify the effect your project has on the success of your business—and ensure that it is a success. You can continue to manage projects as you have in the past, but if this book can teach you one thing that you did not know about formal project management tools and methodologies, isn't it worth it?

Exercise:

What IT projects are either on the horizon or currently underway in your organization? Identify any anticipated or current challenges with the projects in the space below. Get into the details of each project. Use a separate sheet of paper if needed. Don't skip this or any other exercise, because all the exercises are designed for your benefit.

As you proceed through this book, look for ideas and suggestions on ways to prevent or deal with the problems you identified. Consider preventive actions over problem resolution. Good project management emphasizes prevention. Dealing with problems that arise is inevitable, but time and money is saved through preventing as many problems as possible. Studies show that the cost of dealing with problems could be as much as 100 times more than the cost of preventing them. The tools and techniques of project management described in this book will help you prevent or reduce problems on your real-world projects.

The book is written to be read sequentially. Each chapter builds on the content of the prior chapters.

Each chapter focuses on a specific component of project management. The text explores the component's role in the overall project management methodology. Each chapter provides a foundation for understanding the value of each component. Some companies may be more disciplined than others in the use of project management methodologies. Our goal is to illustrate that there is substantial value in each component, and that a rigorous application offers the greatest value to a company. Each chapter wraps up with a couple of questions to consider as they apply to your own organization.

As you read this book, you are encouraged to take advantage of the numerous additional features we have included to make your learning more fun.

 ## Interactive Web-Based Content

RMC has created a special Web site (www.rmcproject.com/IT) specifically for readers of this book. Throughout the text, you will be invited to share your ideas and experience on a number of project management topics with other readers of this book. On the Web site, you will also have access to printable templates of forms used in this book, and additional tips, tricks, and articles relating to topics discussed here.

Key Terms

Throughout this book, you will see sidebars containing important definitions that will enhance your project management learning experience.

 ## Tricks of the Trade

This book will teach you many tricks of the best project managers, indicated by this Tricks of the Trade® icon.

Applying It in the Field

This icon indicates stories contributed by real project managers. Learn the tricks they have developed in their own careers that make a difference when managing real-world projects.

 ### Quotes from Real-World IT

This icon designates relevant quotes from the IT professionals interviewed for this book. Their complete interviews can be found in Appendix C.

Exercises

Each chapter has exercises for you to complete to reinforce the concepts discussed in the chapter. The exercises will help you determine what you know and do not know, and what you might need to spend more time focusing on. We encourage you to complete all the exercises.

At the end of each chapter, you will find the following topics:

Throughout the Project

Many of the concepts introduced in this book are first used during the early initiating or planning stages of a project. However, the concepts are woven throughout the project. This section of each chapter will walk you through the application of the concepts as they apply throughout the project.

Team Members

Project management activities are not performed by just the project manager; they are done with the help of team members. Therefore, each chapter includes a section about how team members should be involved in a project. Understanding the team members' roles and activities within a project aids in improved communication and the building of strong project management teams.

Chapter Summary
Key Concepts

A summary of key concepts at the end of each chapter is designed to reinforce the learning experience.

Questions for Discussion

Considering each chapter's end questions will take you from the theoretical context of the book into your own business environment. The objective of the questions is to ensure you understand the material well enough to make that transition. These questions are also designed for use in university and college courses based on this book.

Action Plan

At the end of each chapter, you are given the opportunity to make notes on how you will apply the concepts learned in the chapter to your current project management efforts. Don't ignore this important idea. You will see immediate rewards as you apply what you have learned.

Exercise:

TRICKS OF THE TRADE: No matter how much training or experience you have with project management tools and methodologies, it's important to recognize that you've developed many tricks to aid in getting projects completed. Consider, and note below, YOUR tricks. As you work through this book, you will be reminded to add to this list at the end of each chapter. Imagine the difference the new tricks will make on your projects!

My Tricks for Managing Projects

My Tricks for Managing Projects

Goals of This Chapter

Upon completion of this chapter, you should be able to:

- Identify, in the proper order, the steps of the project management process

- Define the project life cycle

- Define and understand the dynamic role of a project management plan

- Identify key project constraints

- Explain the science and art of project management

- Understand the role of IT in business

- Explain how IT-centric processes complement project management methodologies

Project Management

A systematic process used to initiate, plan, execute, monitor and control, and close a project to meet defined objectives

It is a science and an art

A project manager was telling a group of people about a great success he recently had on his project. The project was the installation of a major telecommunications system. "You should have seen my team on this project! When two major pieces of equipment needed for this system were delivered, we discovered there was no place to store them until they were installed. Instead of having a nine-day delay from returning the equipment and having it redelivered when we were ready, we were able to find a place to store the equipment nearby after only two days of searching!"

Exercise:

How would you feel if you were this project manager? Would you feel on top of the world? Would you feel you deserve a raise or promotion?

Was the project successful? Why or why not?

Answer:

If you thought you would feel great and should get a raise or a promotion, then you missed something important. The project manager should have been fired, not promoted. Look at the story again.

You should ask, "Why didn't he realize he needed a place to put the equipment?" The project manager certainly worked miracles, but he focused his expertise on dealing with the problem, rather than preventing it!

Don't get started in project management by making the mistakes other project managers do. A project manager's job is not to deal with problems, but to prevent them.

The Science of Project Management

If you look at projects from a company perspective, projects cost money, time, and resources. A project that has gone awry has the potential to negatively impact the company's reputation and earnings. Consider also the rapid, volatile changes in the global marketplace brought on by technology and the Internet. You can see why it is critical to accomplish work faster, cheaper, and easier.

What about the personal perspective? Are you overloaded with projects right now? Do you KNOW you will be successful on each one? Do you even know how success is defined for each one? Do you have a plan for managing each one?

From both a company and a personal perspective, the science of project management is needed. Imagine a project manager who needs to move a lot of baggage from one place to another. She tries a number of potential solutions, none of which are ideal or efficient. Eventually she invents a wheel that allows her to move the baggage quickly and efficiently. She goes into town with her invention and discovers that everyone else is already using a wheel. A simple story, but that is how many project managers operate; by reinventing the wheel. To avoid reinventing the wheel of project management, project managers need to realize there is already a science of project management. All they need to do is adapt it to their projects and their organizations.

The science of project management is the systematic process of initiating, planning, executing, monitoring and controlling, and closing a project. Project management does not mean "wing it."

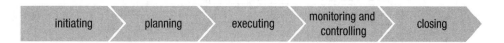

Rita's Process Chart

The following chart was developed by Rita Mulcahy, and is included in her book, *PMP® Exam Prep*. It has been used by people around the world to understand the project management processes quickly and effectively. This real-world process applies to both large and small projects. Depending on the size and scope of the project, each step may take only a few minutes or possibly several days.

INITIATING	PLANNING (This is the only process group with a set order)	EXECUTING	MONITORING & CONTROLLING	CLOSING
► Select project manager	► Determine how you will do planning—part of all management plans	► Execute the work according to the PM plan	► Take action to control the project	► Confirm work is done to requirements
► Determine company culture and existing systems	► Finalize requirements	► Produce product scope	► Measure performance against the performance measurement baseline	► Complete procurement closure
► Collect processes, procedures, and historical information	► Create project scope statement	► Request changes	► Measure performance against other metrics determined by the project manager	► Gain formal acceptance of the product
► Divide large projects into phases	► Determine what to purchase	► Implement only approved changes		► Complete final performance reporting
► Understand the business case	► Determine team	► Ensure common understanding	► Determine variances and if they warrant a change request	► Index and archive records
► Uncover initial requirements and risks	► Create WBS and WBS dictionary	► Use the work authorization system	► Influence the factors that cause changes	► Update lessons learned knowledge base
► Create measurable objectives	► Create activity list	► Continuously improve	► Request changes	► Hand off completed product
► Develop project charter	► Create network diagram	► Follow processes	► Perform integrated change control	► Release resources
► Identify stakeholders	► Estimate resource requirements	► Perform quality assurance	► Approve or reject changes	
► Develop stakeholder management strategy	► Estimate time and cost	► Perform quality audits	► Inform stakeholders of approved changes	
	► Determine critical path	► Acquire final team	► Manage configuration	
	► Develop schedule	► Manage people	► Create forecasts	
	► Develop budget	► Evaluate team and project performance	► Gain acceptance of interim deliverables from the customer	
	► Determine quality standards, processes, and metrics	► Hold team-building activities	► Perform quality control	
	► Create process improvement plan	► Give recognition and rewards	► Report on project performance	
	► Determine all roles and responsibilities	► Use issue logs	► Perform risk audits	
	► Plan communications	► Facilitate conflict resolution	► Manage reserves	
	► Perform risk identification, qualitative and quantitative risk analysis, and risk response planning	► Send and receive information	► Administer procurements	
	► Go back—iterations	► Hold meetings		
	► Prepare procurement documents	► Select sellers		
	► Finalize the "how to execute and control" parts of all management plans			
	► Develop final PM plan and performance measurement baseline that are realistic			
	► Gain formal approval of the plan			
	► Hold kickoff meeting			

As you review the elements of the chart, ask yourself, "How much of what is listed here do I know? How much do I do? What do I still need to understand?"

Note that this is not a process for doing the work (e.g., design, code, test; correctly called the project life cycle) but rather a step-by-step process for managing projects (the project management process).

It is important for you to understand the primary focus of each step in the project management process. We will not cover the details of each of them here. Remember that the big things that will make the most improvements on your projects are described in this book.

Note also that a product may involve projects to create it, projects to market it, and projects to improve it. Each of these would make use of the project life cycle and project management processes.

Initiating

The first step in project management is initiating. Initiating defines the high-level objectives of the project and the business rationale for the project. What problem are we trying to solve? Initiating is the process of understanding precisely what we are being asked to do. This process gets everyone off on the same foot, with the same level of understanding of the problem and project definitions. The initiating process opens the door to ask questions and obtain clarity from the project sponsor. The initiating process includes identifying constraints and limitations such as budget, time, and interoperability issues. The result of the initiating process is an approved project charter, which will guide the rest of the project, and identification of stakeholders, whose needs must be incorporated into the project.

Planning

Planning takes the overall objectives defined in the initiating process and expands them into a detailed plan. Planning is a key element of project management. Expect to spend a substantial amount of time in the planning process. This is where the project team will walk through the work of the project. With a solid plan in place, project execution should go more smoothly. In some industries, planning could take 60 percent of the length of the project time!

Project Life Cycle

What you need to do to DO the work (e.g., designing, coding, testing, etc.)

Product Life Cycle

The life cycle of a product from conception to retirement

Project Management Process

What you need to do to MANAGE the work (initiating, planning, executing, monitoring and controlling, and closing

The focus of planning is to save the project time and money, and to improve your personal brand within the company. It is important to keep in mind that planning will help determine whether you can be successful. The end result of the planning process is the creation of a project management plan; a roadmap with measurable milestones for the whole project. In the interviews in Appendix C, notice that the project managers regularly come back to the planning output documents to ensure the project is on track, to identify areas of risk, and to measure the impacts of any change requests against the original project management plan.

Project planning is iterative—as the project evolves, many of the initial plans may need to be modified or expanded.

Executing

Executing is the process of putting the project management plan into action. The purpose of the executing processes is to complete the work defined in the project management plan. The project manager's role is to make sure the work gets done according to the plan, and the end dates and budgets are met. The focus is on completing the plan.

Monitoring and Controlling

To control means to measure the project's performance. In the controlling processes, the project manager measures project performance against the plan. Measurements are analyzed, and adjustments to the project; changes, corrective actions, and preventive actions, are identified and implemented to assure that project objectives are met.

Closing

Closing is when the project manager ties up all the loose ends. At project closing, the project manager conducts a final review of the plan to make sure everything that was committed to in the initiating and planning stages has been finished. The project manager must confirm that the goals and objectives of the sponsor, customers, and stakeholders have been met. Document the team's and the project's success in a final report. Determine what information from this project might be useful to help make your next project easier. Wrap up the administrative functions including closing out the accounting records. And, archive the project files for future reference. Throw a party to celebrate the project's success.

Follow the Whole Process

Project managers are often thrust into a project that is already underway. The new project manager must take the time to review the project management plan and ensure it is clearly understood, not only by him or herself, but also by all of the team members responsible for executing the plan. If the plan is not clear, it is time to return to the initiating and planning processes. A clear project management plan that is built on a solid understanding of the sponsor's, customers,' and stakeholders' needs, will help ensure a successful outcome.

One of the key objectives of taking a scientific approach to project management is to prevent problems that could derail the initiative. Utilizing project management methodologies shifts time from when the work is being done (executing and monitoring and controlling) to planning. Initiating and planning activities prevent problems later and save time. These activities are not optional. Jumping into a project without following the flow of the project management methodology is asking for trouble.

Another important point to remember, which is emphasized in the interviews in Appendix C, is that project management is iterative. That is to say, as a project progresses, the proactive project manager will repeat many of the planning activities as more and better information about the project is uncovered.

Project Constraints

A project manager needs to manage all aspects of the project, not only time and cost. Project constraints also include risk, scope, quality, resources, and customer satisfaction, as illustrated in the following graphic. One aspect of the project can affect the others. Examples of constraints may include the date a milestone or the project must be completed or the maximum allowable risk a project may have. Constraints are used to help evaluate competing demands.

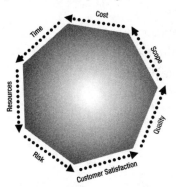

Make certain that all constraints are prioritized by the project sponsor. The project manager uses this prioritization throughout the project to properly plan the project, evaluate the impact of changes, and prove successful project completion. It is important to realize that a change to one constraint should be evaluated for its effect on all of the other constraints. In other words, it is unlikely that you can shorten the schedule without causing a negative impact on cost, risk, etc.

 "The goal of project management is to deliver the best solution for the client's business. This may require some changes in the original scope. The sooner these change requirements are recognized, the faster they can be addressed, and the lower the impact on the project."
–*Ronald Nickell, Senior Project Manager, PMO, CM2HILL*
Read the complete interview with Ronald Nickell in Appendix C.

It is the responsibility of the project manager to integrate all of the aspects of the project, pulling them together in order to produce successful outcomes.

The Art of Project Management

The art of project management addresses HOW project managers use the science of project management. How do they acquire realistic estimates from those who will do the work? How do they ensure the schedule is really agreed to and bought into by everyone? The art of project management involves more than just people skills.

The art of project management includes skills such as:

Leadership
- Influencing the organization to get things done
- Planning for the future
- Strategizing alternative plans and actions
- Prioritizing issues and alternatives
- Being oriented to the big picture
- Driving toward achieving objectives
- Delegating
- Building the team
- Motivating the team
- Rewarding performance
- Being aware of how politics affect the project and attempting to mitigate negative impacts

- Having financial know-how
- Setting performance standards
- Delegating technical work to experts on the team
- Trusting and respecting team members and their contributions

Creative Problem Solving
- Being innovative, thinking outside the box
- Solving the root cause problems rather than the problems as first presented
- Organizing the project, processes, and people

Communication
- Clarifying issues and objectives
- Managing relationships with everyone
- Resolving conflicts
- Negotiating
- Knowing what and how to communicate
- Managing communications
- Giving feedback

Project Management from an IT Perspective

The role of IT is to install, maintain, and monitor hardware and software systems so that a business can run more efficiently and cost effectively. The IT infrastructure and its applications support business processes from multimedia communications to customer service to supply chain management. It doesn't matter what method a company uses to leverage IT, whether built out in-house, with the use of a service provider, in the virtual environment of cloud computing, or in some combination. What matters is that the IT environment is managed as a holistic environment designed to support the firm's goals, objectives, and strategy.

It is critically important to recognize that IT, by itself, should not be a cost center. To support IT as a business enabler, every device, every application, every change in service delivery should be viewed as part of a total technology solution for the organization.

Accelerated Project Management

Project management in the IT environment occurs on an accelerated basis due to the organization's dependency on the network

The Accelerated IT Project Timeline

The IT organization leads a very high-profile life because IT is a business enabler. The slightest glitch in e-mail, and the help desk phones start ringing off the hook. If a core business application is inaccessible, the trouble ticket escalation process kicks into high gear. Everyone in the company is inextricably linked to the network. As a consequence, IT lives under a microscope, being viewed by everyone in the company at all times. Any substantive changes or modifications to the network almost always occur in the evenings and on weekends. The reason for this: No one in the organization can get their job done when the network is inoperable. We have come to be wholly dependent on the network, even accessing it remotely from our smart phones and home computers.

In managing projects in the IT environment, the initiating/planning/executing/ monitoring and controlling/closing project flow must take place, but it is accelerated due to the firm's dependency on the network. Employees must be able to access all of their tools, all of the time, whether they are customer-facing or not. Order entry systems, backup and recovery processes, and application access, whether at the desktop or in the cloud, all feed into knowledge bases that are the lifeblood of the company. All components of IT are tightly linked to all the other business components. Changes to one area will impact other areas.

IT projects are also accelerated due to the competitive advantage they can afford an organization. When a Web presence became critical in the early 1980s, IT was responsible for getting the Web site set up. The developers had to be forward thinking, because in rapid succession online ordering coupled with security was next, then integration with back-end systems for customer support and database mining, then integration with communication technologies for online support, until today, when you go to a Web site and a pop-up window appears to offer a contact center agent available to assist you immediately! It is this rapid succession of additional opportunities that drives IT project acceleration. Companies that cannot keep up with the pace lose customers to those that can.

The Impact of Changing Technology

An important part of the art of project management is managing the expectations of the people associated with the project (stakeholders). Consider the Web site scenario and how quickly it moved from being a portal to obtain information to being an interactive site. As a project manager, how is it possible to keep up with that level of rapid change? We will get into this in substantially more detail in Chapter 5, but the net of it is that IT project managers can meet accelerated timelines and rapidly changing expectations by taking large projects and breaking them down into smaller, more manageable components.

Changing expectations can be tightly controlled when the project manager focuses on smaller incremental projects. Issues regarding integration and interoperability are addressed in the initiating and planning processes. Limitations or constraints are also identified in this early stage of the project. Review the elements in Rita's Process Chart in the Initiating and Planning columns. The importance of spending ample time in the initiating and planning processes cannot be overemphasized.

Moore's Law says that technology improves exponentially approximately every two years. This means that no matter where a project manager is in a technology implementation, some component critical to the project's success will undoubtedly have a better/faster/cheaper alternative during the course of the implementation. That is a serious impact. What should an IT project manager do?

Project management is a closed-loop process, with progress review opportunities built in. Ongoing review allows the project manager to accommodate new and better information into the project management plan. It also allows for the accommodation of different technologies that would better solve the problem being addressed by the project.

Consider a situation involving the telephone. A few years back, the telephone performed a handful of simple functions. It rang. It provided voicemail. It provided a light to tell you when you had voicemail messages. Today the telephone on a desk is capable of providing not just a phone call; it can also provide video of the caller, multiple lines that connect for audio conferencing, and even applications to tell you the weather or to place an order for products. That simple desk phone evolved to a sophisticated computing device that also links to your e-mail and mobile phone.

Imagine you are a project manager in the executing process of rolling out new desk phones. You discover a better, albeit more expensive, option to the standard handset. Ignoring the new phones would not be a good idea. Ignoring the phones opens the door to the company's competitors being able to take advantage of the new technology. Changing phone models across the board would have a serious fiscal impact on the project's budget. This is the perfect time to look at the project management plan and have a frank discussion with the project sponsor. Questions to consider in the review would be:

- Would the additional investment in the new phones produce measurable benefits?
- Do all workers need the new phones?
- Are there some workers for whom the new phones would produce substantial benefits?
- What are the training requirements to maximize the adoption of the new phones?
- What criteria would the team use to identify those workers who would benefit from the new technology?
- What are the implications of not investing in the new technology?
- What other infrastructure components would need to be upgraded or replaced to make the new technology operational?

These are just a few of the questions an IT project manager would have to consider midway through the current project. An iterative project management plan allows the project manager and the team to be vigilant regarding optimizing the existing installed technology and taking advantage of emerging technologies.

Process Improvement Standards for IT: Six Sigma, ITIL, Kaizen

As we have noted, information technology is tightly integrated, evolves rapidly, and is fundamental to business operations. In an effort to retain control of the entire IT environment and ensure ongoing interoperability, several IT-specific, standards-based process improvement methodologies have been developed. Organizations that use IT-centric process improvement methodologies understand the value defined methodologies bring to the situation. IT-specific process improvement methodologies are complementary to project management methodologies. Organizations that use both IT and project management methodologies have grasped the value good process definitions bring to the company, including faster, better execution, enhanced results, and improved company performance.

There are a variety of standards-based process improvement methodologies including Six Sigma, ITIL, and Kaizen. Six Sigma and Kaizen have ties to W. Edwards Deming's continuous improvement philosophies. All of these process improvement methodologies are commonly perceived as IT-centric project management. Six Sigma is aimed at narrow slices of technology, while ITIL and Kaizen are broad and encompassing. There are strengths and weaknesses for an organizations to consider when selecting one type of process improvement methodology for IT over another. The two most commonly implemented standards for IT are Six Sigma and ITIL.

For more information about these models, please see Appendix A.

Team Members

The role of team members in the project management process is explained throughout this book. It is important to recognize that everyone has projects; therefore, everyone needs to understand the fundamentals of project management methodologies. All team members should:

- Understand the project management process
- Know their role in each step of the project they are engaged with
- Have clear assignments of work—what is expected and when it is due—plus clear assignments of any reporting, meetings, or other activities required of them on the project
- Push back when they feel it is necessary
- Provide technical advice; be the technical experts
- Perform the work in the project management plan

As individual members of a larger team, each member is responsible to the overall team to ensure the project's success. Every team member must be willing to:

- Tell the truth
- Ask for help
- Contribute ideas
- Take responsibility
- Be accountable
- Compromise

Team members are empowered to:

- Participate in learning what needs to be done, when, and how their pieces fit into the project
- Find better ways to meet the project objectives
- Realize how their work impacts other team members and the success of the project

TRICKS OF THE TRADE Have your team help you create "ground rules" for your project.

....

TRICKS OF THE TRADE Involve your team in planning the project so it becomes their project too.

....

TRICKS OF THE TRADE Throughout the life of the project, review progress as part of team meetings.

....

Chapter Summary
Key Concepts
Project management:

- Is proactive
- Is a science and an art
- Is a systematic process
- Involves balancing all project constraints

Project management for IT:

- Is accelerated
- Is subject to changing expectations
- Is subject to rapid changes in technology

Process improvement methodologies for IT include:

- Six Sigma process improvements
- ITIL
- Kaizen

Questions for Discussion
What is included in the "science" of project management?

What is included in the "art" of project management?

What makes project management for IT particularly challenging?

Action Plan

1. What will you do differently in your real-world project management as a result of reading this chapter?
2. Add new items to your personal Tricks list in Chapter 2.

What Action?	Why?	By When?	Who Will Be Involved?	Who Will Be Affected?	Status

Goals of This Chapter

Upon completion of this chapter, you should be able to:

- Define what is a project charter

- Give examples of soft and hard metrics of a project

Project Charter

A formal document recognizing the existence of the project

It may be created by the project manager, but is issued by the sponsor in the initiating process

It defines the high-level requirements for the project and links the project to the ongoing work of the organization

Have you ever been asked to do a project, only to discover that the project did not have support of upper management and had a high probability of being cancelled? Are cancelled projects a common occurrence in your organization? To gain support and cooperation for projects, a project manager must obtain a project charter that has been signed off by the project's sponsor.

The project charter, developed in the initiating process of a project, is a formal document issued by the project's sponsor that authorizes the project and the project manager. A project charter dramatically reduces the risk of a project being cancelled due to lack of support or perceived value to the company. It documents the overall objectives of the project and helps manage the expectations. Think of it as a target for the project. The document needs to be broad enough so it does not need to be changed, as the project evolves. If the project charter is changed, the changes have to be approved the sponsor.

A project charter is owned by upper management and/or the project sponsor. The charter gives the project manager and his or her team the high-level scope, schedule, and resource window from which to operate. If events change those overall parameters, the sponsors must be contacted and approve the actions.

It is important not to confuse the project charter and the project management plan. The charter is owned by the executive sponsor. The project management plan is owned by the project manager. The project planning process, covered in depth in the following chapters, expands the project charter to a detailed project management plan Any deviations to the plan that are still within the overall window of the project charter can be handled by the project manager and the project team. Many times, however, project sponsors are included in the decision-making process to manage expectations and to give early warning of events that could at a later time impact the charter parameters.

What Is Included in the Project Charter?

The project charter includes fundamental information used to authorize and establish the basis for a project. The charter justifies the project in terms of its value to the company.

Project Title and Description This section includes a simple, high-level description of what is the project. For example, the description may be to upgrade all existing TDM-based desk phones to IP telephones; or to implement softphones on all sales personnel laptops.

Project Manager Assigned and Authority Level This section names the project manager and states whether he or she can determine, manage, and approve changes to the budget, schedule, staffing, etc. The charter gives the project manager authority to make use of company resources to complete the project and may be a big help on projects when authority must be used to gain cooperation.

What a project manager is given authority to do is very company-specific. Some companies allow the project manager to select resources; others require the sponsor to be involved. Some companies allow the project manager to come up with a detailed schedule that meets a requested end date. Others are not concerned with a required end date and let the project manager tell them how long the project will take.

Business Case This section of the charter explains what business problem is being solved with the project. It addresses the question of why the project is being undertaken. The project manager needs to know this, as he or she will need to make many day-to-day decisions, keeping the business case in mind.

Resources Preassigned In this section of the project charter, the sponsor identifies how many and what resources will be provided for the project. Some projects come with a limited number of human resources available or with some team members preassigned. Some team members may need office space, computers, or other capital expense items. Some team members may be in a different geographic location, impacting the project it different ways than a wholly localized team.

Stakeholders This is the sponsor's impression as to who are the stakeholders. Stakeholder analysis comes later in the project management process.

Stakeholder Requirements as Known This section of the project charter identifies the high-level requirements related to both project and product scope. Known stakeholder requirements are the requirements that have been used to justify the project. Further work to clarify and finalize the requirements will come later.

Product Description/Deliverables This section includes the project sponsor's indication of what specific product deliverables are wanted, and what will be the end result of the project. It is important to have a clear picture of what constitutes the end result of the project. Is it a report on an emerging technology or a network upgrade? Should the report include recommendations to implement the technology, or is it limited to fact gathering? A measure of project success is that all the deliverables are met.

Measurable Project Objectives This section addresses how the project ties into the organization's strategic goals, and includes the project objectives that support those goals. The objectives need to be measurable and will depend on the defined priority of the project constraints.

Soft metrics are typically difficult to quantify. If you receive a project charter with only soft metrics, consider it a red flag for needing to establish solid metrics prior to beginning the project. Alternatively, by adding hard metrics to a soft metric statement, the metric can become more meaningful. Hard metrics have a unit of measure (e.g., a percentage of change, a specific dollar value, a unit of time).

Examples of soft metrics include:

- Improve client satisfaction
- Increase product quality
- Improve process flow
- Increase employee productivity
- Improve information flow

Examples of hard metrics include:

- Increase in sales by a defined percentage
- Reduce costs by a defined percentage or specific dollar amount
- Reduce product production waste by a defined percentage
- Reduce manufacturing time by a defined period of time on a per unit basis

A project manager should encourage the project sponsor to convert soft metrics. Instead of "increase product quality," try using "reduce defective products by [a defined percentage.]" Instead of "increase employee productivity," consider using "increase the number of calls handled by each contact center agent by [a defined percentage], allowing us to handle more calls with the existing staff."

Notice in each of the interviews in Appendix C how different metrics are used when developing the project charter. The key "ah-ha" that spans all of the interviews is that the metrics selected for a project's charter are selected specifically to support the company's bigger vision or strategy. This was consistent whether the firm was vertically market-centric, conducting internal IT projects, or implementing IT projects for an external customer.

Project Approval Requirements This section identifies what items need to be approved for the project, and who will have sign-off. The question "What designates success?" is answered.

High Level Project Risks Potential threats and opportunities for the project are listed here. In-depth risk identification occurs later in the planning processes.

Signature and Approval The charter requires a signature from the project's sponsor. The signature is necessary in order to give authority and make the project official. Depending on the environment in which your project will be completed, there could be more than one signature necessary on the project charter.

Project Charter

Project Title and Description (*What is the project?*) **Customer Satisfaction Fix-It Project**

Over the last few months, the quality assurance department has discovered many of our customers' orders for our XYZ equipment have taken the customer ten times longer to place through our computer network than our competitors' networks. The purpose of this project is to investigate the reasons for the problem and propose a solution. The solution will be authorized as a subsequent project. Quality Control has detailed records of their findings that can be used to speed up this project.

Project Manager Assigned and Authority Level (*Who is given authority to lead the project, and can he/she determine, manage, and approve changes to budget, schedule, staffing, etc.?*)

Jan Navratil shall be the project manager for this project and have authority to select team members and determine the final project budget.

Business Case (*Why is the project being done? On what financial or other basis can we justify doing this project? Describe the project purpose and justification.*)

This project is being completed in order to prevent a further breakdown of customer satisfaction. We expect that improved customer satisfaction will increase revenue to the company in the first year by at least $200,000 due to a decrease in service calls. As a side benefit, we hope that the project will generate ideas on improving customer satisfaction while fixing this problem.

Resources Preassigned (*How many or which resources will be provided?*)

Steve Peterson and Julie Dirksen are already dedicated to the project because of their expertise in computer networks of this type. Other resources will be determined by the project manager.

Stakeholders (*Who will affect or be affected by the project (influence the project), as known to date?*)

Stakeholders include Jason Craft representing Quality Control, Jennie Rutter in Customer Service, and Eric Rudolf in Marketing. These resources are available to assist the project as needed by the project manager.

Stakeholder Requirements As Known (*Requirements related to both project and product scope*)

Attached to this document are the detailed specifications for the existing system, the requirements that the existing system was designed to meet. It is expected that this project will not change how the system affects the existing requirements.

The project must include utilizing the data available from Quality Control.

Product Description/Deliverables (*What specific product deliverables are wanted, and what will be the end result of the project?*)

1. A work breakdown structure, due within two weeks, that outlines the plan for accomplishing the project, followed one week later by a list of risks in completing the project.
2. A report that outlines what can be changed, how much each change will cost, and the expected decrease in the time it takes to place an order resulting from each change. Few words are necessary in the report, but it must be created electronically and be agreed to by the representatives for Quality Control, Customer Service, and Marketing, in addition to the project team.
3. A list of the interactions with our customers necessary to complete the changes.

Measurable Project Objectives (*How does the project tie into the organization's strategic goals? What project objectives support those goals? The objectives need to be measurable and will depend on the defined priority of the project constraints.*)

The objective of this project is to improve customer satisfaction by reducing the time customers spend placing orders via the computer network to 10 percent of the current time. Scope and customer satisfaction are the top priorities on this project, closely followed by schedule and then cost.

> ► **Summary milestone schedule:** Due no later than September 1, 20XX.
> ► **Summary budget:** U.S. $50,000.

Project Approval Requirements (*What items need to be approved for the project, and who will have sign-off? What designates success?*)

Approvals for this project include:
> ► The sponsor will approve the WBS before planning efforts continue.
> ► The sponsor will approve the list of risks before planning efforts continue.

Final project approval will be determined by the sponsor.

High-Level Project Risks (*Potential threats and opportunities for the project*)

> ► Because this project analyzes customer satisfaction, the project may help generate ideas to improve customer satisfaction, resulting in higher levels of customer retention.
> ► Because we have little experience in this area, implementing an inadequate solution could cause more frustration and more time delays for customers, resulting in additional lost business.
> ► Because this problem is greatly troubling to our customers, project delay could result in lost customers, jeopardizing the likelihood of meeting this year's sales goals.
> ► Because assessment of this system is difficult, changes to the system could affect the requirements the system was designed to meet, resulting in impacts to other business functions.

Project Sponsor Authorizing This Project:

_____	_____
Connor Mulcahy, Executive Vice President	Kerry Mulcahy, Vice President

Sample Project Charter

Do not underestimate the value of the project charter. The project charter is such an important document that a project should not be started without one. If the project charter serves as a definition of how success will be measured, then without a project charter, the project and project manager cannot be successful.

A project charter provides, at a minimum, the following benefits:

- Formally recognizes (authorizes) the existence of the project, or establishes the project—this means a project does not exist without a project charter
- Designates the parameters within which the project manager has the authority to operate
- Gives the project manager authority to spend money and commit resources
- Provides the high-level requirements for the project
- Links the project to the ongoing work of the organization

A project charter is needed because:

- It ensures the project manager understands the sponsor's needs
- It provides key information needed to get started
- It provides a reference document to make sure everyone is on the same page later in the project
- It provides the basis to plan the project
- It empowers and protects the project manager by describing what he or she is being asked to accomplish

Exercise:

What's Wrong with This Picture?

Using what you have learned in this chapter, analyze this sample project charter.

Project Charter
Project Title:
Move all of the in-house contact center agents to home-based offices
Project Manager Assigned:
Contact Center Director
Goal:
To complete the transfer of personnel in 90 days
Business Case:
Home agents will be happier and thus will be able to resolve more customer calls
The company real estate expenses will be reduced
Product Description:
Transfer contact center agents out of corporate offices into home-based offices
Signed and Approved By:
Crystal Clearly (Contact Center Director)

Answer:

The project charter has a title, but no detailed project description.

The project manager is assigned, but what exactly is the contact center director going to do on this project?

The goal is to complete the employee transfer to home offices in 90 days, but what happens if the agents have small children at home? How will supervision of the agents be handled?

Are there any assumptions or constraints?

Does this project have financing? Who is responsible for setting up the home offices to OSHA standards?

This product description does not give enough details to know what is and is not going to be included in the employee transfer. What are the deliverables? What are the due dates for the deliverables?

Crystal Clearly is one of the sponsors, but if the entire contact center team of agents is being transferred, human resources, IT, and the telephony team should also be included as sponsors.

Exercise:

Create a project charter for your real-world project.

Project Charter		
Project Title		Project Manager
Project Description		
Project Manager Authority Level		
Business Case		
Resources Preassigned		
Stakeholders	Stakeholder Name	Stakeholder Requirements
Product Description	Describe the features & functions of the product of the project	
Deliverables	List the deliverables below	
	Deliverable:	Due date:
Measurable Project Objectives		
Prioritized Constraints	Number according to priority (1 is highest, 7 is lowest)	
	Time:	Cost:
	Quality:	Risk:
	Customer Satisfaction:	Resources:
	Scope:	
Project Approval Requirements		
Risks Known at This Time		
Sponsor Signature	Signature	
	Printed Name	
	Date	

Throughout the Project

The planning process will determine if the project can be completed within the confines of the project charter. Any changes to the project charter must be approved by the signer of the project charter. Any change to the project charter can affect the entire plan for completing the project (e.g., the cost, schedule, and risks for the project) and should be considered a huge change to the project.

 "After you have identified the project, try to find every possible thing you can do to draw out the information and get it down on paper. It will give you a very good idea of exactly what it is going to take to get it complete."
–*Abe McCallum, CEO, Clikthrough, Inc.*
Read the complete interview with Abe McCallum in Appendix C.

During the life of the project, stakeholders can easily lose track of what the project is trying to accomplish. Here are some tricks for using the project charter to prevent this from happening.

 The project manager can use the project charter to remind everyone involved on the project exactly what the project is. It is a great help in preventing or limiting scope creep.

 Have the project charter graphically designed (so it looks official). Then send color copies to all stakeholders and team members' bosses to post on their walls. This keeps the focus on what is the project, and therefore what is not in the project, thereby preventing some scope creep. It will also keep team members reminded of the project, making them more apt to complete their work assignments.

 Design the approved project charter to be used as a screensaver by all team members throughout the project. This keeps the project in the minds of the team members, and serves as a visible reminder to all who see it that an important project is underway.

Scope Creep

Work unofficially added to the project that is outside of the defined project objectives

Review the charter with the team members at team meetings one-third and two-thirds of the way through the project in order to keep them focused on the project. Not only will this prevent some scope creep, it will also help the team see if they are off track.

Team Members

Team members' role in the project charter can include:

- Review the project charter when they are assigned to the project
- Provide feedback on the project charter to make sure it is complete and understandable
- Make sure all the work they do falls within the project charter
- Evaluate any requested changes to make sure they fall within the project charter
- Reread the project charter during the project to keep it in focus

Chapter Summary
Key Concepts
A project charter:

- Is a high-level target for the project
- Authorizes the project and the project manager
- Must be approved before project work begins

Project charter metrics:

- Must be measurable
- Are often used to determine project success

Soft metrics are:

- Difficult to measure
- Broad, open statements

Hard metrics are:

- Easily measured
- Specific and precise
- Used to justify the business value of a project

Questions for Discussion
Why should a project manager NOT begin a project without an approved project charter?

| |
| |
| |
| |
| |

Describe the fundamental information included in a project charter document.

How can the project charter be used during completion of project work?

Action Plan

1. What will you do differently in your real-world project management as a result of reading this chapter?
2. Add new items to your personal Tricks list in Chapter 2.

What Action?	Why?	By When?	Who Will Be Involved?	Who Will Be Affected?	Status

Incrementalization: Breaking the Work into Projects

Goals of This Chapter

Upon completion of this chapter, you should be able to:

- Identify what is a project

- Define incrementalization and the importance of its application to project management for IT

- Be able to break a project down into its component parts that can be planned, managed, and controlled

- Identify the differences between project, program, and portfolio management

- Explain real options analysis for IT project management and how to apply it

- Understand the Value Matrix

Imagine the following situation. Your boss walks into your office and says, "The system is not functioning properly. I am giving you a project to find out what is wrong and asking you to fix it. I need the work done by June 25th, and I can assign you only four people from our company to help." Is this a project?

Think again. Many aspects of this story may be familiar to you, but does the situation describe a project?

IT project success is critical to every organization. However, all too frequently we take on elephant-sized projects without a defined roadmap. This is a recipe for disaster. If we agree that projects are a cornerst one of business growth and success, then we need to handle projects with an eye toward efficient execution, building each succeeding project on the success of the prior initiative. This is incrementalization: the process of breaking down a large project into manageable initiatives. Collectively, the IT project roadmap provides long term, sustainable, competitive differentiation. Each succeeding initiative makes it increasingly more difficult for competitors to catch up or leapfrog the organization.

Project

Work that creates a unique product, service, or result

It is temporary—it has a beginning and an end

It has interrelated activities

Incrementalization

The process of breaking down a large project into manageable initiatives

Defining a Project

A project has a beginning and an end with measurable milestones integrated into the project management plan. The desired result or expected outcome is known and clearly defined at the onset, before work is even begun on the project. Though an end was not described in the "Figure out what is wrong and fix it" directive, one can assume that asking a few exploratory questions might clear up what is the final objective. A defined outcome for this scenario might be: "This project will be completed when the system is working up to the performance level achieved prior to the problem."

Another characteristic of a project is that it can be organized into logical execution blocks with a defined beginning, middle, and end. A real project supports the IT manager's ability to commit to an end date and/or an end budget.

If your answer to the opening scenario is, "I always have this situation thrown at me," then perhaps you have been missing something important. In fact, most project managers have a similar response. The answer to the scenario question of: "Is this a project?" is that it is not just one project. It is at least two projects!

Each project needs to be staffed and scheduled and an end date or time needs to be agreed to by the stakeholders before project executing begins. You cannot estimate or schedule "fix it" until you know what is wrong with it. Therefore, the scenario involves least two projects, "Figure out what is wrong" and "Fix it." This is an example of incrementalization; taking an undefined large project, breaking it down into its respective key issues, and then defining the parameters for each project.

For every "project" supplied by management, the customer, or any other source, the project manager must look at the assignment and break it down into appropriate projects that can be planned, managed, and controlled. The project manager and the team can then stake their reputations on being able to successfully complete the project, which has defined end dates and budgets that the team agrees it can meet. Breaking the work down to manageable projects helps to properly plan each project.

The Key to IT Project Success: Starting Small

Think of starting small as the agile method of project management. Your goal as a project manager is to be fast, efficient, and effective. You want to be quick hitting, impactful, and build on prior successes. This is the value that incrementalization will bring to your projects.

Consider the typical enterprise, composed of dozens of departments and hundreds of workgroups. Each of these workgroups has defined multiple workflows. In many cases, these flows span the entire company, such as e-mail and voicemail. However, there are other flows that are specific to a team, such as performance management or on-boarding training to human resources; or skills update training to the technical support team.

Each workflow can be automated to varying degrees, and even put in the cloud for anytime, anywhere, any device access. The project associated with moving the workflow into the cloud is justified by immediate time and cost saving benefits. However, without a project manager overseeing all of the IT initiatives, the integration of the various projects has the potential for going awry due to a myriad of reasons.

Horizontal Incrementalization

Horizontally incrementalized projects are those that cut across multiple departments. These projects would be associated with service delivery, customer care, engineering, and others. These projects typically involve investments that are larger and systems that are more complex than those applied to discrete workgroups. The risk of failure and cost of implementation for IT and the firm are much higher. For example, the e-mail application is a workflow across all workgroups. Everyone needs and uses it. Project management in this complex environment would require a stepped approach within targeted workgroups that make up the collective horizontal workflow. The project manager breaks the project into manageable, rapidly executable components. An effective project manager, then, makes the end result, smooth workflow across multiple departments, much larger than the sum of the individual parts (the workflow within each individual department).

Vertical Incrementalization

In a vertical incrementalization, the project manager is working within a single workgroup or department. For example, the collaborative team may start with one work process such as document management for version control, then add remote desktop management to support geographically distributed teams, allowing the team to tap into resources throughout the firm no matter where they may be physically residing. The net result for one team is readily rolled out to additional teams as the executing process has been streamlined through the closed feedback loop. This is an important point to consider as more and more firms are moving toward dynamic, fluid, collaborative teams.

Exercise:

Apply what you have learned by trying these examples. How would you break the following work into projects?

Work	Potential Projects
Determine if a new enterprise computer application could be created and then create it	
Improve an existing document sharing application	
Implement video conferencing across six regional offices	

Answer:

This is no one right answer to this exercise. Below are some project solutions we developed for the exercise. See how your projects map to ours.

Work	Potential Projects
Determine if a new enterprise computer application could be created and then create it	• Analyze requirements • Design the new computer program • Create the new program • Test the new program
Improve an existing document sharing application	• Determine why the old application needs improving and suggest improvements • Study the feasibility of various product improvements and determine which improvements will be done • Implement the improvements • Field test the improved product • Roll out the improved product

Implement video conferencing across six regional offices	• Analyze the impact on the wide area network • Analyze the impact on the local area network • Develop detailed infrastructure upgrade designs • Acquire the equipment needed for additional bandwidth • Acquire the equipment need for video conferencing at two sites • Run the test-bed between the sites • Adjust WAN and LAN specifications based on test-bed results • Roll out the solution across remaining four sites

Did you think that the bullets provided were parts of one project, rather than the titles for many projects? To be successful on large projects, the work must be organized into logical phases or smaller projects that can be planned from start to finish with a realistic and agreed-upon schedule and budget. The "projects" on the left side of the table cannot meet these requirements, while the projects listed on the right side can.

 To determine how many projects you really have, consider the following questions:

- Does the work have a defined beginning and end?
- Can you feel confident in your end date and end budget for the project to the point of staking your reputation on them?
- Will you use substantially the same resources for completing all the work?
- Do all parts of the work have the same focus and the same primary deliverables?

If you said no to any of these questions, you have more than one project.

What Is a Successful Project?

Completing all the work of the project:

- On time
- Within budget
- With an acceptable quality level
- With an acceptable risk level
- With stakeholder satisfaction

What Is a Program?

Program

A group of interrelated projects managed in a coordinated way

A project that is too complex or has been identified as potentially taking a long time cannot easily be managed, and has a propensity to go over budget and underdeliver on value. It would be better to break it down into smaller projects or to call the "project" a program with many project components. A program is a group of interrelated projects managed in a coordinated way. The projects can be managed together as a program, or they can be planned and managed separately. To convert a large project into its respective components, consider a phased implementation. Phases could include feasibility, design, code, test, implement, turnover, and on-going support and maintenance. Each phase is planned and managed individually, making each component a smaller, separate project. By breaking complex projects down, they become easier to manage and control, thus increasing the probability of success.

Project Portfolio Management

Portfolio

A group of programs to achieve a specific goal

May otherwise be unrelated

A portfolio can generally be described as a group of programs to achieve a specific strategic business goal. The programs may not be related other than the fact that they are helping to achieve that common strategic goal.

Are you familiar with the 10 percent rule? It goes like this: For any company asset, only about 10 percent of the value or functionality is utilized. Observe the way the average person uses a given application, then watch a power user with the same application. The net result of the 10 percent rule is that the true return on assets for the organization is substantially lower than what the consultants and salespeople tell you it will be.

This rule can be applied to projects within an organization. The solution to the 10 percent rule is a project manager that oversees the entire IT project portfolio. This project manager sees exactly how each and every initiative contributes to the overall goals and objectives of the organization. This uber project manager, just like an investment counselor, is responsible for managing and optimizing the IT investments of an organization, thereby reducing duplication and increasing productivity across the entire enterprise.

When a company seeks to make IT a business enabler, IT project management is an interactive, engaging activity. Every small project rolls up into a program. Each project program then rolls up to the larger business objectives and should map to the overall business strategy of the company. Before anyone takes a single step toward project planning, the project value must be determined relative to other project opportunities in a value matrix. By managing IT projects in this manner, every application, service, tool, or device deployed can be justified. Conversely, employees considering deploying rogue tools because "they prefer them" are stopped before they can do any measurable damage to the company, its reputation, brand, or goals. Stopping rogue tool deployment saves money by ensuring only approved tools that integrate with each other are used. An approved products, tools, and applications list ensures everyone in the company is working toward achieving the company's vision and objectives in the most cost-effective, efficient manner.

What Is the Value Matrix?

The Value Matrix is a concept that was introduced in 2000 in a book by Amir Hartman and John Sifonis: *Net Ready* (2000, McGraw-Hill), to provide a tool for use in prioritizing IT projects. The value matrix measures projects on two dimensions: business critical and innovative/newness. The value matrix, while rather subjective, allows project managers to weigh projects relative to each other. The matrix allows the project manager to determine which projects need to be implemented first based on the organization's objectives. If the company is pursuing cost reduction and profitability, then those projects that fall along the business critical axis would take priority. If the company is pursuing a strategy of innovation, then those projects that support that goal would take precedence.

Notice in each of the interviews in Appendix C, how the organizations have elected to prioritize their portfolio of IT projects. ETG, Clikthrough, and Sungard Higher Education prioritize based on ROI and profitability. These firms would align their projects along the business critical axis. CH2M HILL, seeking to break into new markets such as alternative energy, would align its projects along the innovation/newness axis.

- Organization or business criticality initiatives are typically focused on productivity and profitability. They answer the question: Does this initiative deliver cost reductions or improve efficiencies?
- Innovation/newness projects are initiatives that are new or innovative compared to others in the marketplace. Projects that have a high degree of innovation/newness are typically focused on competitive differentiation and growth.

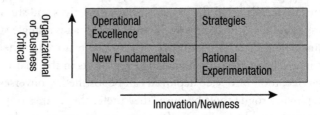

Using Real Options Analysis to Queue Up the Next Program

Real options analysis (ROA) is a decision modeling process used to determine what the next investment should be. When applied to project management, it helps guide decision makers and the project manager in determining the order in which competing projects, the rollup into large complex programs, should be executed. ROA provides a method of valuing each program in terms of future benefits.

The value of ROA as a decision model is that it takes into account uncertainty and volatility of the parameters of a program and management's ability to respond to the evolution. The challenge in developing a real options decision model comes in determining just how volatile the program's value will be upon completion. For example, the rapid decline in the global economy in the fourth quarter of 2008 would have substantially increased the value of projects that emphasized efficiencies and cost reductions; however, no one could have predicted just how rapid the decline would be. Therein lays the technical difficulty of the volatility measure.

Even with the difficulty in determining the volatility measure, real options decision modeling is a more accurate measure than net present value (NPV). This is especially true the larger the program in size and time. As we have noted, the longer the project timeline, the higher the likelihood of running into hurdles. NPV is only capable of modeling uncertainty by using predetermined management decisions within specific, independent scenarios, and then equating the project value on a per-scenario basis, hoping for the outcome to be somewhere in line with the scenario producing the highest project value.

In the real world of business, management retains the right to change their mind based on the most current data available. ROA outputs reflect this business fluidity in a more precise manner. The ROA decision method, however, is still an attempt to predict the future, and as a consequence, the end results are only as accurate as the quality of the inputs.

The bottom line to ROA decision modeling is that the more volatile or risky the program is, the higher the future value needs to be to justify execution relative to other programs in the portfolio.

Team Members

Managers, as well as team members, should have training in project management. When this is the case, it might be management or the sponsor who breaks the program into acceptable projects, rather than the project manager. Trained team members might also see the project from a perspective different than the project manager's. They may suggest that the project needs to be broken down further than what has already been done.

 Throughout the project, it is smart to make sure that you reevaluate and that you have adequately broken the work into projects.

 Projects that undergo a substantial number of changes may indicate a need for the project manager to reevaluate if the breaking of the work into projects is still appropriate.

Chapter Summary
Key Concepts

A project:

- Is temporary and unique
- Has an agreed-upon end date and budget
- Has one focus

A program:

- Is a group of interrelated projects

Incrementalization:

- Reduces large projects to a manageable size aimed at fast and efficient project execution

A portfolio:

- Is a group of projects or programs that collectively map to a specific strategic goal

A value matrix:

- Measures projects on two dimensions: business critical and innovative/newness

Questions for Discussion

What are the advantages of breaking a large project into several related projects (a program)?

How can you tell if your "project" is really more than one project?

How can you determine if a project maps to your organization's goals and objectives?

Action Plan

1. What will you do differently in your real-world project management as a result of reading this chapter?
2. Add new items to your personal Tricks list in Chapter 2.

What Action?	Why?	By When?	Who Will Be Involved?	Who Will Be Affected?	Status

Gaining, Creating, and Using Historical Data

Goals of This Chapter

Upon completion of this chapter, you should be able to:

- Explain why and how a project management knowledge base can be used to continually improve project implementations

- Identify what type of project data is most beneficial to capture, and how to capture it on an ongoing basis throughout a project

- Engage the project team in providing positive and negative project closure feedback

How does an organization achieve continuous process improvement with its project initiatives? Put another way, how does an organization refrain from repeating flawed project plans?

An organization can continue to improve its project initiatives by keeping records of past projects and making this knowledge base available to all of its project managers. Historical information is the body of documents that makes up the project management knowledge base.

By reviewing the history of IT projects in the organization, a project manager can quickly see how the newest initiative fits into the overall strategic plans of the company. In addition, the project manager is able to identify and repeat successful methods and learn from the mistakes of others. By reviewing historical project records, the IT team is able to take industry standard process improvement frameworks such as Six Sigma or ITIL and add its own best practices unique to the company to achieve increasingly greater IT implementation efficiencies.

Historical Information

Records from past projects, used to plan and manage future projects, thereby improving the process of project management

In addition, historical information offers project managers the opportunity to:

Improve Estimation Metrics Estimating project resources is a challenge. Historical project data of projects similar in size and scope will improve estimation metrics because they are concrete. People tend to be optimistic about their ability to accomplish tasks. A quick look at your own to-do list will illustrate that optimism. Historical data curbs that optimism, offering fact-based data.

Reuse Effective Techniques Project history reports identify and document successful strategies, techniques, shortcuts, and checklists. For example, stop filling every team member's inbox with documents and communications, when a centralized repository for everything related to a project, accessible by all team members, has been proven to be a better technique.

Employ Templates for Similar Activities Every project is unique, but there are many activities that are repeatable across most projects. Take advantage of repeatable WBSs, resources, costing profiles, and identified potential risks. Using proven historical data as a foundation, a template for a budget spreadsheet with net values inserted can give a project a substantial jump in the initiating and planning processes of a similar project.

> **Caveat Regarding Templates:** Project templates of WBSs, contracts, and other documents are valuable pieces of historical information. However, it is important to note that templates provide only a starting point. The project manager must customize the templates to address each specific project's unique requirements.

REAL WORLD IT "Our project management application allows us to save each and every project as a template. Then you can just build off that template. That's part of what we do. We also have documentation on our network about statements of work, RFPs, and all the other customer project-related materials."
—Jay Helms, vCIO, Evolution Technology Group
Read the complete interview with Jay Helms in Appendix C.

Exercise:

Describe the type of information you will need to collect before beginning a project.

Answer:

- How the project fits into or supports the company's strategic plan
- Contracts, if the work is done under contract
- Local and national government regulations
- Likely stakeholders and team members
- Past relationships with the sponsor of the project, likely stakeholders, and team members
- A list of people who may be good team members
- What is currently going on in the company
- Other current projects
- Basic information from past projects including:
  - ▸ Templates
  - ▸ Work breakdown structures
  - ▸ Estimates for each work package in work breakdown structures
  - ▸ Lists of risks
  - ▸ Lessons learned documents
  - ▸ Project schedules

The collection of historical information obviously depends on the project. The more important the project, or the more perceived risk in the project, the more time should be spent collecting this information. Once you get beyond the basics, great project managers might even collect information including:

- Past history with the customer
- Past history of the resources on the project
- Information about personal relationships between any of the stakeholders that could affect the project
- Stakeholder risk tolerances
- Data regarding how the company's organizational structure has positively or negatively affected past projects
- Information about how past projects and their successes might affect the current project
- All e-mails and meeting minutes from before the project was approved, including e-mails to and from the customer
- Any articles written about similar projects in trade journals, professional magazines, or even local newspapers
- Technical and project management literature containing articles, ideas, problems, and solutions related to the project type
- Technical drawings, specifications
- Organizational charts
- Resumes of potential team members
- Reports from the marketing or sales department
- A description of what kinds of decisions the project manager can make on the project
- A list of official or unofficial experts who can assist the project team and the customer in identifying scope, risks, managing the project, etc.
- Priority of this project compared to all others in the organization
- Information about relevant cultural issues and suggested protocol, documentation, language barriers, and social customs
- Data about key players for the team and the customer:
  - ▸ What are their stated objectives?
  - ▸ What are their hidden objectives?
  - ▸ What are their areas of influence?
  - ▸ What are their weaknesses?

- Thoughts of the experts and boss on how to complete the project
- Thoughts of the experts and boss on potential problems or problem areas

Collecting historical data will decrease project problems, and your project will take less time to plan and manage.

Throughout the Project

Throughout the planning and executing of your project, you will uncover useful information, create new processes, and make discoveries that will not only improve your project, but could be useful to others. Document these items as they are learned. By recording key performance measures such as estimates against actual costs on an ongoing basis, the project report and historical information file is built along the way. This saves substantial time at the end of the project when the sponsor is looking to receive all of the project information. Compiling this information, as well as the project management plan, work breakdown structure, and other documents associated with the project, concurrently builds the historical information file. Archiving the historical file allows other project managers to benefit from the information.

Quantitative measures to record as part of the project history file:

Costs Include the project spreadsheet for all costs associated with the project. The spreadsheet should show the estimated costs of the project and final costs at project completion. Note the delta between the estimate and actual costs for each item. Include an explanation if the delta is substantial.

Project Schedule The project history file should include major milestones, estimated dates, and actual dates. The project schedule should also show who on the team was responsible for each of the deliverables. Any deviation between the project schedule dates and the actual delivery dates needs to be explained.

Scope Any changes to the project scope, either expansion or contraction, need to be identified with an explanation of who requested and authorized the changes. In addition, impacts of the changes in scope on other project constraints should be included in the documentation.

Lessons Learned

What was done right, what was done wrong, and what should be done differently on similar future projects

Lessons Learned

The historical information file needs to contain a final report based on the team's project debriefing. The debriefing session takes place soon after the project is completed in order to capture critical feedback while it is still fresh in the minds of the team. The report should focus on lessons learned while implementing the project. The lessons learned document should include recommendations for future projects.

Obtaining feedback, especially negative feedback, can be a challenge for even the best project manager. Use a blend of techniques to obtain as much feedback as possible for the historical records. Identify issues that came up in the project and the actions required by the team to get them resolved and to keep the project on track. Discuss ways to prevent those issues from arising in future projects. Credit the team with being aware of and responsive to the issues and preventing them from negatively impacting the project

It is awkward to criticize the project and the team in front of the group. However, criticism can be constructive and beneficial. Therefore, it is important for the project manager to provide a method for submitting anonymous feedback throughout the project. Prior to milestone deliverable review sessions, remind the team of the ability to submit issues and suggestions anonymously and the method to do.

The CH2M HILL and Sungard Higher Education interviews in Appendix C have several good ideas for conducting lessons learned meetings. At the top of the list is to clearly state that the participants need to treat each other with respect. This is not a gripe session, but a way for everyone on the team to learn and grow. Another key response in the interviews is that it is the project manager's responsibility to ensure everyone on the team contributes to the discussion. Some companies use a round-robin method, continuously going around the table giving each person an opportunity to voice a specific thought until participants have nothing further to contribute.

Other tips for conducting a successful lessons learned session include:

Meeting Agenda Always have a meeting agenda and send the agenda to the team several days in advance of the meeting. An agenda provides a venue to lay ground rules for the meeting such as no personal attacks, and keep comments constructive and relative to the project. An agenda also helps to keep the meeting focused and on track, making the team more efficient.

Record Assign someone familiar with the project to be the meeting recorder. The meeting notes should be transcribed and distributed to the team. This communication keeps everyone on task and focused on the project and their role within the team.

Use Open-Ended Questions Start the discussions by identifying what worked well. This gets everyone thinking in a positive manner about the project. Rephrase negative questions to obtain constructive input. For example, rather than "What didn't work well?" try "What could we do better?" or "What would you recommend we do differently on future projects?" How a question is phrased is important for keeping the tone of the meeting constructive.

 Contributed by: Lisa Harper, PMP
Cleveland, OH

After holding several lessons learned sessions at the end of projects, and not getting the needed attendance or the needed feedback, I came up with the following tricks for my lessons learned sessions:

The first trick is to ensure a high-level executive attends the session. It is generally not difficult to get the commitment of the executive that benefited most from the project. Some executives will even offer to provide opening or closing comments during the session. This trick increased my participation to 100 percent. Plus, the executives really appreciate being invited.

The second trick is to create an assignment for the meeting. Provide instructions to the participants one to two weeks prior to the session. The assignment is to create a presentation. Give them the option to team up with someone. Provide a template that lists "what went right," "what we could have done differently," and "what I learned." The most important piece of the instructions is to tell them to have fun! This trick increased the quantity and quality of data collected for my lessons learned sessions. You should see some of the creative PowerPoint presentations the teams have come up with. This also gives individuals the opportunity to utilize their presenting skills that they might not otherwise get.

I have received so much positive feedback from these sessions that I made this a standard practice on all my projects.

"It is very important to sit down at the end of the project, and take the appropriate extra time with everybody on the team and have a discussion about how the project went from everybody's point of view. Whether that's the tester who was at the tail end of the project or the requirements analyst who was at the front end of the project, or the salesperson who sold it. It is not a matter of gaining one point of view; it is a desire to gain a comprehensive view. On every project, everyone must provide feedback because when we do, collectively we continuously improve upon the process."

–Ronald Nickell, Senior Project Manager, PMO, CM2HILL

Read the complete interview with Ronald Nickell in Appendix C.

 "The sessions are not about blame, they are about learning. So if the mission or project didn't go exactly as planned, you take off your project hat and come into a room where there are no levels, no hierarchies and just evaluate, for the sake of learning, what happened. In this way, if we do a similar project, the next time we know what to do differently."

–Alice Ferone, Associate Director for Global Business Services (GBS),
The Procter & Gamble Company

Read the complete interview with Alice Ferone in Appendix C.

Team Members

Team members' role regarding historical information can include:

- Provide the project manager with any historical information to which the project manager may not have access
- Review historical information and make use of it on their parts of the project
- Continually look for historical information that may be of use to the project
- Collect data on the current project to be included as historical information for future projects

Chapter Summary
Key Concepts
Historical information:

- Includes records from past projects
- Helps avoid repeating mistakes of previous projects
- Improves project process efficiencies
- Is collected throughout each project

Benefits of historical information:

- Reuse effective techniques and templates
- Improve estimation metrics
- Learn from past mistakes

Effective lessons learned sessions:

- Provide a method for anonymous feedback
- Always follow an agenda
- Use open-ended questions
- Start on a positive note

Questions for Discussion
How does historical information benefit a project manager?

| |
| |
| |
| |
| |

What are some good sources of historical information?

List some ways in which a project manager can obtain team member feedback on the project.

Action Plan

1. What will you do differently in your real-world project management as a result of reading this chapter?
2. Add new items to your personal Tricks list in Chapter 2.

What Action?	Why?	By When?	Who Will Be Involved?	Who Will Be Affected?	Status

Identifying and Managing Stakeholders

Goals of This Chapter

Upon completion of this chapter, you should be able to:

- Develop a list of stakeholders for your project

- Be able to conduct a stakeholder analysis

- Explain the business value of a recognition and rewards system

- Understand the value of maintaining an issue log

The term "stakeholders" encompasses everyone involved with or affected by the project, plus those who can positively or negatively affect the project. Stakeholders on a project can be a project manager's best friends or worst enemies.

Stakeholders are driven by their wishes, fears, goals, and personal agendas of a project. Understanding the motivations of each stakeholder is important to the success of the project, especially if a stakeholder holds a contrarian point of view.

For example, in addition to internal stakeholders, a technology project that could potentially eliminate a large number of jobs, such as moving a call center off-shore, may also involve state and local government officials. Political entities prefer to keep high paying, clean technology positions within their jurisdiction. These stakeholders would therefore represent a contrarian position on the off-shoring of the firm's call center.

Stakeholders may include:

Sponsor This person authorizes the project, provides the funding, supports the project, and promotes the project's value throughout the management team as well as across departments and divisions.

Management This category includes any company management other than the sponsor or functional managers.

> ### Stakeholders
>
> People and organizations involved in or impacted by the project
>
> People and organizations that can positively or negatively impact the project

Project Management Office This is a centralized group whose roles within the organization may include providing policies, methodologies, and templates for projects, providing support and guidance to others, and/or providing and overseeing project managers.

Project Manager The project manager is responsible for the ongoing project activities and uses project management to manage the project.

Functional Managers These individuals manage departments within the performing organization. There are often numerous functional managers involved in IT implementations, including network administrators, wide area network managers, software managers, and security managers.

Team Team members are responsible for executing the project management plan. IT project teams are generally made up of a cross section of the technology group.

Customers The people inside the organization that have requested the project are its customers. The customers provide the project scope and approve scope changes.

End Users Those people who will use the product of the project are its end users. End users can be the entire organization, as in a project involving changing e-mail applications, or can be a subgroup, as in a project where a new application is being added to the customer relationship management (CRM) suite for sales and contact center personnel.

Public This term includes anyone who may be affected by the project. Public stakeholders can be political, environmental, or the community in which the company is located. For example, politicians and the community have a vested interested in keeping jobs local, so any project that seeks to move jobs elsewhere will be met with resistance. The other side of that coin is excellent publicity when a company seeks to grow its local presence and add jobs. Environmentalists as stakeholders come into play when a company is making claims of being green, polluting/cleaning up the air or water, or increasing/decreasing its carbon footprint in its production process.

Funding Sources Funding sources can include banks, governmental, or outside agencies. Any firm that provides substantial financial resources to a company is a stakeholder in the project associated with the funds. Most projects are funded internally, but there are opportunities to obtain outside funding, which increases the organization's and the project's visibility. Outside funding might come in the form of tax breaks from the State and County to move a business into the community. Investment capital is another source of outside funding obtained through private equity or merger/acquisition. Additional sources of outside funding include government grants; cooperative research projects such as those being developing around alternative energy between universities and government; or test-bed funding such as the Boulder SmartGrid project, which is a cooperative of numerous technology companies.

Most project managers fail to identify and properly involve some important stakeholders on their projects. This is another value of reviewing historical project information, being able to identify stakeholders not top of mind.

Stakeholders will have different roles in the project depending on their level of influence and the relationship of their role to the project. The telephony team will have a greater role in a distributed contact center project than the IT director. The technology security team will also have a greater role in the same project than the internal networking team. Stakeholder roles are fluid and dynamic, depending on the project. In one project, an individual stakeholder may be highly influential and, in a different project, much less so.

Stakeholder analysis, discussed later in this chapter, will help project managers in managing stakeholders and their competing needs.

Exercise:

Apply what you have learned about stakeholders with the following scenario.

An old (legacy) system has been negatively impacting the performance of three projects within a company. The legacy system is used in the accounting department and the finance department to create reports for financial analysis that are critical for company business decisions. The negative impact on the three existing projects is estimated to be greater than the cost of replacing the legacy system; therefore, company management has approved a project to create a new system to replace the legacy system. All projects in this company are required to follow company project, quality, and risk management standards.

Stakeholder (by name)	Level of Influence 1 to 10 (10 is highest) The project manager and team need to define what each level of influence means so that all are evaluating it by the same criteria or measure	What will make them satisfied? (What are their requirements and expectations?)

Answer:

The key to any stakeholder list is to make sure all of the right people are included. In this example, many people overlook the team who created the legacy system. What if the team members are still working with the company and do not want their work to be replaced? Could this team get in the way? Could this team provide additional insight into how the legacy system impacts other systems and processes within the company?

How about the departments whose standards the project must follow? They will need to ensure the standards are adhered to, and they should be looking for the project to provide any suggestions for improving the standards.

The scenario says the legacy system was used to make critical company decisions. When identifying stakeholders, you might ask yourself, "What decisions?" "Who is making them?" and "What actionable information and data points are they using to make these decisions?" Why not ask those who use the data what they wish to see the new system provide while the "determine requirements" project is ongoing and before the "implement the requirements" project is started?

Key stakeholders almost everyone forgets are the project managers for the three other projects who have been negatively impacted by the legacy system. Wouldn't they have some insight into what the new system should and should not do? Could they provide historical records of past problems with the old system? Should there be some interface between these projects?

Based on the exercise scenario, the stakeholders would include:

- Creators of the legacy system
- Owners of company standards
- Those who will be using the system to make critical company decisions
- Project managers for the other projects
- Sponsor
- Team
- Project manager
- Project management office (if one exists)
- Management
- Accounting department
- Finance department
- IT department

The following items are tricks to help you with stakeholder identification.

 When an entire department is really a stakeholder, a trick is to have one person from the department WIN the opportunity to represent the department on the project. Such work is worthy of being on a resume (curriculum vitae), and that stakeholder will participate more fully, having won the position.

 If identifying all the stakeholders is so important, how do you know if you have identified them all? Try this trick. Ask each stakeholder who they think the stakeholders are for the project. You are guaranteed to find more stakeholders.

 Instead of asking, "Who are the stakeholders?" ask people who they think would most benefit from the project and who they think might be able to provide advice. Also, it is interesting to ask in confidence who the stakeholder thinks does NOT want this project to succeed, or "Who might get in the way of the completion of the project?" Reframing the question can bring out different responses.

Stakeholder Analysis

Not only is it important to determine early in the project who all the stakeholders are, by name, it is important to make sure you know how much they can influence your project, and what will make them satisfied. Stakeholder analysis helps the project manager to plan how he or she will manage the stakeholders involved in the project. Stakeholder analysis yields information on each of the stakeholders, their relationships to the project, interests in the project, and expected outcomes. A comprehensive analysis of the stakeholders will assist the project manager in constructing the optimal approach to the project and its challenges, and will enable better negotiations and communications with each of the stakeholders. It is helpful to know that Fred in Finance is unable to compromise with Sam in Sales; or that Arthur in Accounting wields tremendous influence throughout the company.

Some stakeholders will need to be involved in establishing the project scope. Some stakeholders might have expectations that have not been put into requirements for the project, which will need to be discovered. Some stakeholders will need to be included in the project reporting cycle, while others will want more frequent and more detailed updates. Some stakeholders will want information transferred to them in a report, and others will prefer a quick e-mail or telephone call. The bottom line: Stakeholders need to be identified by name, and their specific needs documented, to the fullest extent possible.

Estimate Each Stakeholder's Level of Influence

Each stakeholder will have influence on the project. Some stakeholders will have substantial influence while others will have a nominal amount of influence. Throughout the planning and managing of a project, the project manager may have to juggle the needs of competing stakeholders. Knowing their influence levels will help handle this juggling.

> **Level of Influence**
>
> The degree to which a stakeholder can positively or negatively affect the course of a project

Not all influence is related to job position. Have you ever seen someone with an administrative job title who can spread his or her influence around in order to get things done?

To determine influence, simply put a 1 to 5 rating next to each stakeholder's name. It does not have to be scientific. A guess will do.

Identify What Will Satisfy Each Stakeholder

REAL WORLD IT "After you have identified the project, try to find every possible thing you can do to draw out the information and get it down on paper. It will give you a very good idea of exactly what it is going to take to get it complete."
—Abe McCallum, CEO, Clikthrough, Inc.
Read the complete interview with Abe McCallum in Appendix C.

Achieving stakeholder satisfaction is as much an art as it is a science. It is different from meeting requirements.

Project managers should identify stakeholder expectations, and seek to convert as many expectations to requirements as possible. Expectations are things the stakeholders anticipate will happen to them, their department, or the company as a whole as a result of the project. Expectations tend to be ambiguous, frequently rooted in assumptions and emotions rather than stated requirements. They may be intentionally or unintentionally hidden. Expectations can often be uncovered during the stakeholder requirements conversation.

Expectations include such things as, "I expect this project will not interrupt my department's work," or "I expect the system will be dramatically improved as a result of the project." Naturally, expectations that go unidentified will have huge impacts across all project constraints.

Stakeholder analysis and management requires a lot of work and a lot of thought. There is one overreaching reason it is worth the effort. A stakeholder who is forgotten or ignored in the planning process will make changes to the project later. All projects have some changes, but investing the effort to avoid unnecessary change is prudent. Project changes can impact the total project cost, its schedule, the quality of the final output, and the team's morale. Some studies show that a change made during project executing could cost 100 times more than a change made during planning the project!

Team Members as Stakeholders

TRICKS OF THE TRADE Team members are also stakeholders. The project manager needs to make an effort to determine what will make them satisfied.

It is important to realize that many team members will do things to work toward something they consider positive, or to move away from something they consider negative. The following is a list of reasons a team member may or may not want to be part of a project:

- They have too much other work to do
- The product of the project will solve a problem they have
- The project has high visibility throughout the company
- They are seeking an opportunity to grow their reputation or career
- They want to learn something new
- They want to use their efforts on the project to gain a promotion
- The project work schedule fits with outside commitments
- The project is a stepping stone to more preferred projects

Communicating with Stakeholders

Communication is one of the top problems on projects, but only because it is not managed. The trick is to start thinking at the beginning of the project, when the stakeholders are first identified, about how people prefer to communicate. Some stakeholders would prefer to be called, others prefer to be e-mailed, some may just want a hard copy of a report.

 Ask stakeholders their preferred communication methods. Remember that these preferences may change throughout the project and you will need to make certain that you update your communications management plan accordingly during your project. Chapter 12 focuses on project communications.

The only way to know how each stakeholder prefers to be kept up-to-date is to ask them directly. The project manager needs to think about communication in terms of collaboration. Communication on a project goes from the project manager to the stakeholders and from the stakeholders to the project manager, throughout the life of the project. If the best way to communicate with each stakeholder is not identified, the project manager is simply adding communication problems to later parts of the project. Great project managers are proactive about communication. They learn how each stakeholder wants or needs to be communicated with BEFORE the project starts, and as each new stakeholder is identified throughout the life of the project.

Preventing problems is easier than dealing with them. The work of identifying stakeholders, their level of interest in the project, their objectives, and their level of influence will pay off later in the project when problems such as these are mitigated or resolved quickly with the support of the correct stakeholder:

- Added project changes and delays
- Missed requirements
- Added conflict
- Loss of expertise
- Rework
- Lower quality

Exercise:

Complete the following chart for one of your real-world projects.

Stakeholder	1-5 Level of Influence	What Will Make Them Satisfied?	Communication Requirements

Throughout the Project

Stakeholders should be involved in planning the project and managing it more extensively than you might be doing on your projects. For example, stakeholders may be involved in the creation of the project scope statement and the WBS.

Stakeholders may become risk response owners, and are also involved in:

- Developing the project management plan
- Identifying constraints
- Identifying and finalizing requirements
- Other parts of risk management
- Approving project changes
- Verifying scope

Managing Stakeholders

Now you know who your stakeholders are, and you know what they want. What next? A project manager must continue to do the following regarding stakeholders:

- Identify any new stakeholders, and include their needs in the stakeholder list
- Make sure all stakeholders' needs are met, including those of the team, by including interactions with stakeholders in the project manager's management activities
- Create and use recognition and rewards systems (See more on this later in this chapter)
- Keep track of stakeholders' issues and document their resolution

Identify New Stakeholders

This seems simple, but it is often forgotten by project managers. Continue to use the tricks for identifying stakeholders while the work is being done. Remember that it is harder to identify stakeholders in the beginning of the project, and it is only while the project is being worked on that some stakeholders will be identified.

 Look for new stakeholders every time there is a change requested on the project. This is often how new stakeholders get involved in the project.

 Include an agenda item, "Who are the stakeholders?" at a team meeting partway through the project to help identify new stakeholders.

 When a project acquires new stakeholders, bringing them up to speed on the project status can be time consuming. In addition to sending the newest stakeholders copies of the project reports and providing them links to the project's internal Web site, consider including them in the next team meeting.

Managing stakeholders also includes managing team members. Even the smallest teams require management. How well a project goes reflects on the team members' reputations and careers. If a team member believes the project will be unsuccessful, he will remove himself from as much work on the project as possible so it does not tarnish his reputation.

The project manager has a duty to team members to make sure there is a realistic schedule so the team members can know when they need to complete work on the project. They need to be provided with a rewards system. They need to be asked their opinions and to contribute to the development of the project management plan. They need to help control the project.

The Value of Stakeholder Management

Are some of your stakeholders difficult to deal with? This often occurs because stakeholders have not been properly identified and managed according to this chapter. In the heat of the battle to complete a project, many project managers drop their efforts to manage stakeholders. This usually leads to a decrease in the effectiveness of their project management. Forgetting the stakeholders later is a sign of an inexperienced project manager, focused on dealing with problems rather than fulfilling the main job of preventing problems.

The following are some tricks project managers have used in managing stakeholders while the project is underway.

 A project manager knew that some of the team members felt strongly that certain scope should have been part of the project. Anticipating that the team might continue pressing to get the scope added, the project manager communicated the following at the first team meeting. "During planning, there were a number of suggested pieces of scope that were specifically determined not to be a part of this project. I will be looking for any attempts to add them back into the project."

 During requirements gathering, a stakeholder expressed concern about how much of her staff's time would be needed on the project. While finalizing the project management plan, the project manager contacted her and said, "As you are aware, some of your staff will be needed on this project. I understand your concern in losing some of your team members without knowing when or for how long. I have designed our project's monthly report to clearly show you when and how much of your staff's time will be needed. Will this help you manage your department and minimize the impact of this project on your department?"

Exercise:

You are working on a project with 14 stakeholders who need to be involved and kept updated on the project. As the project manager, what will you do to fulfill those needs?

Answer:

Here are some ideas you may not have thought of:

TRICKS OF THE TRADE Invite stakeholders to some team meetings so they feel they are a part of things and so they can see just how complex some project issues are.

Send a report to the stakeholders describing the things the stakeholders have done to help the project.

 Have a meeting for all of the stakeholders so that they can be updated on the progress of the project and how it might affect them.

 Add your best ideas to our Web site (www.rmcproject.com/IT) and access the contributions of others.

Why bother doing such work? Such actions are proactive and make the stakeholders feel that their needs and concerns are being considered, even if they are not agreed to. These actions also serve the valuable function of keeping open communication channels with the stakeholders. They enable stakeholders to inform you of potential changes, added risks, and other information. Such actions therefore PREVENT problems later and catch problems before they become too large.

Contributed by: Hajisaleh Kutchhi
Pune, Maharashtra, India

This trick could be used for any long-running maintenance project where resource movements are quite frequent. Problems in this type of project often include getting new resources trained as quickly as possible, and the lack of available documentation on application systems. New team members may spend hours looking for information which is urgently needed, in order to fix a problem on the project.

This type of situation can be very well handled by creating a "knowledge repository" for the project. This knowledge repository has A-to-Z information about the project, for new team members to refer to. This knowledge repository thus reduces the effort of experienced/existing project staff towards training the new team members, and enables new team members to work on the various project activities independently.

In particular, the repository includes:

1. Induction and Training Program—Information for a new team member to study.

2. "Induction Checklist"—Items like completion of Induction course, important and "must know" information for the project, i.e., getting various access rights to various systems/functions, etc.

3. Log of issues and defects encountered on the project in the past (particularly frequent defects) and their resolutions and history of actions.

4. "How do I" documents—The processes to perform various project-specific routine tasks required as part of day-to-day activities. Possible examples include; "How do I promote code in so-and-so environment?" "How do I deploy the application?" "How do I set up a new batch job?" "How do I set up so-and-so data?"

5. Contact List—A list of all contacts that may need to be reached for various reasons while working on the project. This may include DBAs, business users, technology staff, staff whose projects are dependent/related to this project, subject matter experts, module leads and managers, production support desk, and other useful help desk numbers.

6. Properly indexed and organized documentation on project domain.

7. Proper documentation on application systems of the project, transaction flows within the system, interface details and any other information which is useful and which is required frequently during the project.

8. Technical manuals which can be referenced when required.

9. Other items as per requirements of the project.

This knowledge repository can be maintained in any shared drive or in a configuration management tool like Microsoft Visual Source Safe, or it can be developed as a stand-alone Web application. Such a repository will make the life of every team member easier and will help in the smooth execution of the project.

Functional Managers as Stakeholders

What about functional managers, those people who "own" or manage resources (people) that are needed for the project? Have you ever gone to them to gain resources and found them uncooperative? If you have been in this situation, think again. To fix or prevent the situation, you should consider why functional managers might be uncooperative.

First of all, functional managers have other work to do, and frequently are not compensated for their efforts to support projects. (Maybe they should be.) Secondly, because many project managers do not properly plan their projects, they frequently ask functional mangers to drop everything to help the project. For these two reasons the problem is the lack of proper project management. In this situation, the problem is not the functional manager, it is the project manager!

"What?" you might say. The solution to dealing with difficult functional managers is to realize that it is the project manager's responsibility to understand the needs of all stakeholders, and to communicate to all stakeholders the schedule for the project in advance. Therefore, there should rarely be an instance when the project manager has to say, "I need resources NOW!" Any time a project manager does this, the individual is, in reality, communicating that he or she is not in control of the project. This is not a good thing for a project manager.

Recognition and Rewards Systems

Expressions of appreciation for the stakeholders and the team members should be built into the project by the project manager. You may be thinking, "Why should I have to reward my team for doing their job?" The long term benefits gained when a quality recognition and rewards system is implemented include:

- Increasing cooperation from those who win and those who do not receive the recognition
- Showing that the project manager appreciates the team's and stakeholders' efforts
- Keeping the team and stakeholders focused on performing in ways that benefit the project
- Keeping everyone focused on what is important to the project
- Creating a positive environment where members will look forward to working with you as a project manager

To create a recognition and reward system, determine how you will motivate and reward not only the team, but also each individual team member. This requires learning what each of your team members and stakeholders want to get out of the project on a professional and personal level.

Below are a few ideas to incorporate into a recognition and rewards system:

- Offer a prize at the project conclusion to the stakeholder who makes the biggest contribution
- Say "thank you" regularly to team members who work extra hours, identify potential problems early, offer suggestions that improve the project's timeline, reduce expenses, or improve the outputs in unexpected ways
- Award prizes such as Team Member of the Month recognition, or cash prizes for exceptional performance
- Recommend team members for raises or choice work assignments, even if such actions by the project manager are not officially part of the team members' performance reviews
- Send notes to stakeholders' managers about great performances
- Plan milestone parties and other celebrations of success
- Acquire training for team members paid for from the project budget
- Adjust the project to assign people to desired or requested activities, or to remove them from disliked activities
- Assign a team member to work where he or she can gain more knowledge

Recognition and rewards should be peppered throughout the project. Small gestures of appreciation, given sincerely and regularly, go a long way to keeping the team motivated and engaged in meeting the project's end product or service requirements.

 Contributed by: V. S. Srividhya
Chennai, Tamil Nadu, India

Based on the core complexity of a project, I design a contest for the team at the planning stage. For example, if it is a testing project, I call it the "Project Tester Award." If it is a Web page designing project, I call it the "Designer Award." I announce the rules for the same and the objective in the project kickoff meeting. The metrics are regularly tracked and I send out notes or make mention of it during status meetings. This promotes healthy competition among the team members and also increases productivity. At the close of the project, when we celebrate our success, I invite important stakeholders and the team to a party. At this venue, I announce the winner of the award. Although there is a single award given, I bring mementos for each and every team member. As they come forward to accept their mementos, I recognize their contributions to the project. Generally everyone loves this. It also serves to make people enthusiastic to work on my next project.

Contributed by: V. S. Srividhya
Chennai, Tamil Nadu, India

When a project team is assigned to me, I get a contact list with each person's name, address, phone number, e-mail address, and their birthday. As the project work progresses, I make it a point to cut a cake for every team member's birthday in our "war room." One person is named as "party planner" and he or she coordinates the party celebrations.

This small but neat trick goes a long way in team building. It also gives the team members a chance to let their hair down and enjoy.

Contributed by: Jackie Labbé, BSc.BM, PMP
Vancouver, British Columbia, Canada

My trick proved quite effective for ensuring some critical studies and documents were completed on time. Since development takes so long in my field, when people are actually at the end there is a big crunch to get all the required studies and documentation in. People are usually tired by this point, and I needed everyone to maintain focus and be energized.

I developed a Lizard Race—a giant sized poster, with pictures of lizards traced out—all leading to the END. A lizard represented a study or document. I then gave each "owner" a rubber lizard from the local toy store. When the "owners" completed their race (meaning study and document approved), they got to go to the race poster, and stick their lizard on it with a rubber band. Then, they ran to my office to collect their reward: chocolate bars for their team! It was fun watching everyone get excited as they participated and watched the race unfold! I would often arrive at my office to find someone waiting with lizard in hand, smiling from ear to ear.

Issue Log

Issue Log

A record used to track issues on the project, their status, and their resolution

It is important for the project manager to document issues as they come up in a project. The issue log is used to keep track of problems and issues that need to be resolved or discussed through the project, the level of urgency, who raised the issue, who is responsible for addressing the issue, and ultimately, how the issue was resolved.

Documentation of how the issue was resolved is a particularly important component. The more detailed the documentation, the more helpful the log will be for future projects that may encounter the same or a very similar issue. The issue log is also an important part of team meetings, project wrap-up sessions, and lessons learned documentation.

An issue log should look like the following:

Issue #	Issue	Date Added	Raised By	Person Assigned	Resolution Due Date	Status	Date Resolved	Resolution

 Keep the issue log in a public place, or post it, so that all stakeholders will know that their issues are going to be addressed, even if the issues are not resolved to their satisfaction. Many people will accept a decision of "no" if they believe their issue has at least been considered.

Stakeholder Management Process

The stakeholder management process should include the following steps:

- Identify each stakeholder by name
- Determine each stakeholder's level of influence on the project
- Assess each stakeholder's knowledge and skills
- Identify all of their requirements, and have the stakeholders prioritize the requirements
- Establish the project outcome that will satisfy each stakeholder
- Determine, manage, and influence each stakeholder's involvement in the project
- Determine and establish each stakeholder's preferred method of communication
- Communicate project information and what they need to know in a timely manner
- Perform ongoing project analysis to ensure the stakeholders' requirements are being met
- Get their sign-off on the project requirements and scope

- Use them as expert advisors
- Use them, where appropriate, in change management and approval
- Keep them engaged in the project by assigning them tasks such as assisting with managing risk
- Involve them in the process of creating lessons learned
- Get their sign-off that the requirements have been met

Team Members

Don't forget that team members are stakeholders too! Team members' roles in identifying and managing stakeholders can include:

- Provide the project manager with their opinions on who are the stakeholders
- Constantly look for missed stakeholders
- Interview stakeholders to determine their expectations, as requested by the project manager
- Assist in managing the issue log

Chapter Summary
Key Concepts
When identifying stakeholders:

- Identify anyone who can affect the project or be affected by the project, both inside and outside the organization
- Determine stakeholders' preferred communication methods and requirements, and what will make them satisfied
- Continue to manage stakeholders and identify new stakeholders throughout the project

Stakeholder analysis and management should include:

- Identify each stakeholder by name
- Determine each stakeholder's level of influence on the project and their requirements
- Determine, manage, and influence each stakeholder's involvement in the project
- Keep stakeholders engaged in the project by assigning them tasks such as assisting with managing risk

The benefits of a recognition and rewards system include:

- Increased cooperation
- Keeping everyone focused on what is important to the project

The issue log provides a central repository of project issues

Questions for Discussion
During which part of a project should you attempt to identify stakeholders? Why?

What is the impact of an effective recognition and rewards system on a project?

| |
| |
| |

What components are included in the issue log and what value does the log provide to the project team?

| |
| |
| |

Action Plan

1. What will you do differently in your real-world project management as a result of reading this chapter?
2. Add new items to your personal Tricks list in Chapter 2.

What Action?	Why?	By When?	Who Will Be Involved?	Who Will Be Affected?	Status

Finalizing Project Objectives— The Project Scope Statement

Goals of This Chapter

Upon completion of this chapter, you should be able to:

- Explain the purpose of a project scope statement

- Explain the difference between product and project scope

- Identify elements that make up the project scope statement

- Explain the business value of the project scope statement

It is of great benefit to the project manager's project, and to his or her career, to think of work relating to scope as, "Making sure all the scope that can be identified is identified in writing, and then managing the project to complete the scope and eliminate the need for unnecessary scope changes." Real project management requires the project manager to know where the trouble spots are and to prevent them from hurting the project. Scope is certainly a potential trouble spot.

This definition of a project manager's work related to scope requires a new way of thinking for many project managers! A project scope statement is one of the most critical components of a project. A detailed project scope statement provides a solid basis for accurate schedule and cost estimates. It is also a detailed documentation of the requirements of all project stakeholders.

Note that this is the generally accepted definition of a project manager's work related to scope. Other recently introduced project management methods use a more iterative approach to scope definition.

Precision Matters

Precision matters in all of the project interactions and documents, but none more so than in the scope document. Consider the impacts of an IT project loosely defined as "Decentralize Contact Center Agents." Now consider the more precise definition for the same project of "Build Out the Technology Infrastructure Required to Support Multi-Media Enabled Remote Contact Center Agents."

Product Scope

The product, service, or result of the project

Project Scope

The work needed to create a product, service, or result (the product scope)

The project scope statement helps to document the project so that everyone involved is aware of what is expected during the project's life cycle. The project scope statement also links the project's objectives with key business strategy and vision. In the previous example, it is clear that the organization desires IT to enable multi-media communication capabilities and enable a distributed workforce. Both of these business goals can readily be incrementally rolled out across the entire company.

The key lesson regarding project scope statements is that each time new scope is added, the ENTIRE project must be reviewed to evaluate the impact of the changes. Added scope might affect risk, cost, time, resources, quality, or customer satisfaction, as well as other work already planned. The impact of a scope change on all of these areas must be evaluated and minimized. For a project manager who understands this, there is no such thing as "Can't we just add this little piece of new work to the project?" Each change can affect many aspects of the project.

There will always be some changes on the project, but unnecessary changes must be prevented, and all changes must be evaluated, documented, and formally approved. To reduce changes in the real world, the project manager will leverage the pre-project stakeholder conversations ensuring that their documented requirements are as complete as possible.

In many cases, stakeholders are extremely busy and may be unwilling or unable to accommodate a sit-down conversation to determine their requirements, especially if doing so requires them to reach consensus with others. It is not unusual for those who have the requirements or scope to not fully understand the technical aspects of the project, nor what it would take to make their requirements happen. They want what they want, and they do not understand why getting it might be so difficult. The key to obtaining complete scope requirements (or time or cost or any other requirements, for that matter) is to keep these thoughts and needs in mind when approaching the stakeholder interviews.

Project managers should approach the process of obtaining requirements from stakeholders with an eye toward the business impact of not receiving a comprehensive requirements list, while recognizing the potential reluctance of stakeholders to formalize their requirements. Consider the following approach.

You might start by stating the following. "This is a challenging project because... so I can imagine the last thing you want to do is to clearly describe in writing all your requirements. However, you are very busy, and you want this project completed by a certain date. I estimate that the project will take up three times more of your time than it should if we do not get all the requirements now. In organizing the project, I will let you know if all the requirements can be completed by that date. But assuming they can, I will need to coordinate cost, resources, quality, and technical issues in organizing this project. I cannot effectively make use of these company resources if I do not have all the requirements. Please, can you take a minute to make sure you are providing me with all the requirements now, before it is too late?"

Depending on who you are talking to, you could be even more assertive by saying such things as, "I know that the last thing you want to do is sit down with the people in your department to finalize your needs. However, if we do not have all your requirements by May 12, I cannot promise that we will be able to accommodate your needs afterward." In other words, the best project managers know that unclear requirements is a potential problem area. They will put the problem "on the table" and specifically address the stakeholders' dislike for completing their requirements.

The best approach for obtaining stakeholder requirements is to clearly explain the balance of the inconvenience of taking the time to provide the requirements up front against the consequences to the project and the company of not taking the time to provide the information.

Look again at the project constraints graphic. Changes later in the project will likely require more time. Another important project management concept, as it relates to scope, is that scope equals cost and time. In other words, the project is planned to accomplish a defined scope for a certain cost or time. If the scope changes, the cost or time should also change!

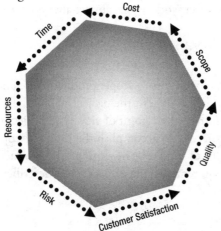

A best practices technique is to ask the stakeholders to prioritize the project requirements. This ensures the project manager is able to accommodate the most important requirements for the project. It also provides a baseline should some of the requirements have to be removed due to resource or other constraints.

Value of Written Communication

Oral communication is prone to misunderstandings. People's minds wander and often they are multitasking, especially when conversing on the telephone. Factor in foreign accents, bad connections, and even basic cultural differences, and effective communication can be a challenge.

A key to eliminating misunderstandings is to insist that project requirements be in writing. The request that requirements be in writing forces the stakeholders to be clear and more complete in their thoughts. It also opens the door for the project manager to ask clarifying questions to obtain a precise list of requirements. Having the project requirements in writing helps the project manager organize and plan the project and all of its components, including measuring how success will be defined. Finally, written requirements support the project manager when a stakeholder seeks to expand the project scope.

In summary:
- Scope must be as complete as possible before planning can start
- Scope must be in writing
- Planning requires integration of scope, time, cost, quality, risk, resources, and customer satisfaction. Scope added later in the project must be evaluated for an impact to other aspects of the project
- Scope added after project work begins almost always causes a resulting schedule change
- Scope must be controlled

As stated earlier, there are two types of scope: product scope and project scope. Product scope describes the product of the project. It is usually created by the customer, or it is written from their point of view. The project scope is the description of the work needed to accomplish the product scope. Both are needed for a successful project. Both should be in writing. The product scope might describe performance requirements; the project scope describes how the project will accomplish them.

To complete the project scope statement, one might perform the following:

- Review what is and what is not included in the project
- Make sure all the stakeholders are identified and requirements are obtained from all of them
- Ask those who provided requirements how complete those requirements are
- Ask those who provided requirements who else might have requirements
- Make sure everyone knows that requirements must be finalized before planning can effectively start, and why this is true
- Make sure the stakeholders' needs, wants, and expectations are turned into requirements

What Is Included in the Project Scope Statement?

There are no templates for project scope statements, as they differ based on the needs of the project. Many of the topics you might consider including are also addressed in the project charter. They are covered from a high-level perspective in the charter. The project scope statement addresses them in more detail.

Product Scope   Overall characteristics of the final approved product of the project

Project Scope   Work the project will do to deliver the product scope or product of the project, as known at this time before the WBS creation

Deliverables   Product and project deliverables

Product Acceptance Criteria   How will you know the products of the project are acceptable

What Is Not Part of the Project   What work is outside the scope of the project

Constraints and Assumptions   Detailed time and cost and other factors that affect scope, as well as detailed lists of what is assumed to be true that may not be true (e.g., the computers will work when turned on, no more than two other projects will be initiated while this project is ongoing)

> **Project Scope Statement**
>
> A document the describes the project deliverables and the work required to create those deliverables

Did you notice:

- How much detail can be included in the project scope statement
- How the rest of project planning will center around this important document
- That this could be one of the most important documents in project management
- That such a document could take time and coordination with stakeholders to complete

Exercise:

What's Wrong with This Picture?

Using what you have learned in this chapter, analyze this sample project scope statement.

Project Scope Statement
IT will upgrade all sales associates' laptops. The upgrade will include new CRM software, wireless LAN connectivity, embedded agents for automated desktop backups, and software to support instant messaging.

Answer:

A project scope statement should contain enough detail for the project manager to know exactly what is included in the project and what is not included. Does the previous project scope statement answer questions such as the following?

- What brand of laptop should be purchased for the sales team?
- Whose budget is covering the expense of the laptops and software?
- What operating system has the firm standardized on?
- When is the technology refresh scheduled to be completed?

- What software manufacturers does the company use for CRM, backups, instant messaging?
- What other software needs to be purchased?
- Does the firm use enterprise licensing, group licensing, hosted software, or software as a service solution for any of the required sales-related software?
- What is IT chartered to do with the older laptops?

Exercise:

Create a project scope statement for your real-world project.

Throughout the Project

When completed, the project scope statement becomes the pivot point to managing scope changes. A comprehensive, written project scope statement will help you determine if changes are within the planned work of the project, and the magnitude of any requested changes. The project scope statement can also be used to remind stakeholders of what is approved scope. The project scope statement document provides a clear basis from which to identify and describe scope changes when they occur.

 On long projects, smart project managers review the project scope statement with stakeholders on a regular basis throughout the project. The goal is to be vigilant in identifying potential scope changes. Finding or preventing scope-specific issues early will help decrease the impact on the other project constraints.

 Contributed by: Miriam Morris
Toronto, Ontario, Canada

When I am defining the success criteria of the project with the sponsor and the team, I always ask them, "How do we set ourselves up for success?" We agree to a short list of SMART (Self-Monitoring Analysis and Reporting Technology) criteria and measures, and I document them in a simple table with 3 columns:

Criteria Description and Measures	Accountability	Evaluation Date
	The accountability shows the name of the person who is accountable for achieving the measures that are deemed successful.	The evaluation date is the date when the success will be measured. This could be end of the project or few months later, when the actual benefits are realized.

I bring this table to the status meetings on a regular basis and remind the team of our agreement on what success looks like. I have found it keeps the team motivated, and it gets us over hurdles when they arise. There is a great feeling of accomplishment when the success is evaluated at the end of the project and we can prove to ourselves that we have been successful. Those who took the accountability on their shoulders at the beginning get the glory... and they want to do it again for future projects.

Contributed by: Srinivas Vadhri
                        Cupertino, CA

I use this trick once the scope and timelines are fully defined and "set in stone," during my weekly communications or for any executive-level presentation. At the bottom of any communication, I include the following statement: "Scope and timelines approved by all stakeholders on ##/##/2010" in a small font. This reminds people, especially project sponsors, that everything is set in stone, and that any changes need to be analyzed against the project constraints.

 Contributed by: Jeffrey Carpenter, PMP
                        Portland, OR

We all know the importance of establishing a change control process with our client and internal team. A good project management team takes care to establish a change control board (CCB), define members, and define a process for identifying changes, categorizing them as defects or enhancements, in scope or out of scope, and then processing change requests. The problem often arises in the execution of this change control process. A project manager may feel bad about "nickel and diming" the client for small changes, particularly at the beginning of the project, so it is common to agree to ad hoc small changes on the fly at no cost without using the formal CCB process.

The problems with this method include the following:
- It starts to set a precedent for how changes will be managed
- Without documentation of the small, "no cost" changes, the client forgets that you accommodated these changes for them —i.e., your goodwill efforts are quickly forgotten
- Unintended consequences can bite you later on
- Little changes can lead to big variances over time

Early in the project, I like to identify some "no cost" small changes, or even a mock change, and run it through the CCB process at the first scheduled internal team and client meeting. This is a non-threatening way to practice the process and, if necessary, revise the process with the client so that it becomes something that is rehearsed and understood. After running through the process, I take time with the client to identify the benefits of the controlled approach to change, as well as scenarios of what could have happened if the formal process had not been used.

Some clients see change control as a negative process associated with more cost to them, and some projects see it as a process that slows down decision-making. Practicing the process up front to work out kinks, demonstrating its value, and getting stakeholders comfortable with using it will serve the project well in the long run.

Team Members

Team members' role in the project scope statement can include:

- Provide feedback on the project scope statement when they are assigned to the team to make sure it is as complete as possible
- Make sure all the work they do falls within the project scope statement
- Help evaluate whether requested changes fall within the project scope statement
- Look for scope creep in the work they do and in the project work they see

Chapter Summary
Key Concepts

Product and project scope must be determined before project work begins

Changes to scope also impact other project constraints

A project scope statement helps reduce unnecessary changes on a project

Communication related to stakeholder requirements should be done in writing to ensure clarity

Questions for Discussion

What can a proactive project manager do to prevent unnecessary scope changes on a project?

What is the difference between product scope and project scope?

Why should stakeholder requirements be in writing?

Action Plan

1. What will you do differently in your real-world project management as a result of reading this chapter?
2. Add new items to your personal Tricks list in Chapter 2.

What Action?	Why?	By When?	Who Will Be Involved?	Who Will Be Affected?	Status

Goals of This Chapter

Upon completion of this chapter, you should be able to:

- Explain how to create a work breakdown structure (WBS)

- Describe the business value of using a WBS

- Understand common problems with the WBS

- Define the elements that make up a WBS dictionary

- Identify the ways a WBS dictionary is used

We don't manage a project. We manage the small pieces. The work breakdown structure is the foundation of everything we do to organize the project. It is created during the beginning of the planning process. It ia also used throughout the project, whenever the scope of the project needs to be reevaluated.

The WBS may look like an organizational chart, but that is where the similarity ends. The WBS is created with the project team from the top of the chart down to the bottom, and serves many purposes:

- By making the project deliverables more precise, the project team knows exactly what has to be accomplished.
- The WBS aids in assigning responsibilities, resource allocation, and monitoring and controlling the project.
- The precision of the WBS aids in improved cost, risk, and time estimates.
- The WBS offers an additional opportunity to confirm with the stakeholders the project's requirements and objectives.

NOTE: The WBS is not the same document as the final schedule.

Work Breakdown Structure (WBS)

A deliverable-oriented, hierarchical structure of work packages that organizes, defines, and graphically displays the total work to be accomplished to achieve the final project objectives

The figure below is an example of a WBS:

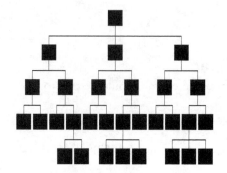

How to Create a WBS

To create a WBS, start at the top by breaking your project into logical, major components which completely define the project. For example, a system development project could break the work into research, conceptual, planning, definition, and evaluation. In addition, most projects add a project management component which includes work that spans all areas of the project.

A WBS focuses on project deliverables (the results of work that needs to be done on the project).

Using the Project Life Cycle Approach

The best way to create the first level is to break the project down by its life cycle.

Taking the life cycle approach in building the WBS provides a foundation for reusing the upper parts of the WBS for other similar projects. Standardized WBSs of similar projects within an organization can aid the tracking of historical trends spanning multiple projects.

Below is an example of the top levels of a WBS for a system development project:

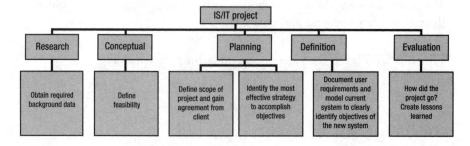

Once the first level of the WBS is created and deemed complete, each of the boxes is tested to see if it needs to be broken down further. Questions like, "Is the work discrete and measurable?" are key. If the answers to these questions are yes, then no further division is necessary. If not, the work is broken down further into two or more smaller pieces. The lowest level of a WBS is called a work package.

Here is an example of breaking down the top level of the WBS, starting with the box identified as "Definition" in the previous WBS example.

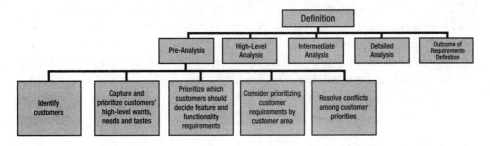

Work Package

The lowest level of a WBS

It contains a collection of work activities that can be assigned to an individual for execution of the work

Work Package Sizing

Just how far should a project manager decompose a project in a WBS? What amount of effort should the work package represent? That depends on the size of the project. Recall from Chapter 5 the concept of incrementalization. The objective of incrementalization is to make projects executable as quickly as possible to build ROI based on project success. Small, fast projects are also much less likely to run into issues with waning interest or departing executive sponsors. By decomposing large multi-year IT projects into smaller increments, the big picture business objectives are substantially more likely to succeed.

The project manager must decide to what level to control the project. Micromanagement is rarely a good idea, but neither is a *laissez faire* management style. The work package size decision is up to the project manager and contingent on the size of the total project. Here are a few rules regarding the work package size:

- Can be realistically and confidently estimated
- Cannot be logically subdivided further
- Is measurable and discrete
- Has about 8 to 80 hours worth of effort (or whatever makes sense for the size and complexity of the project)

- Has a meaningful conclusion and deliverable
- Can be completed without the need for more information
- May be outsourced or contracted

The size of work packages also relates to more precise reporting and project control. Instead of asking the nebulous question of "What percent complete are you?" the project manager can ask, "Are these specific work packages completed yet?"

 To gain the benefits of added control on the project, determine in advance how far off the schedule you can be and still make it up. Then make the work packages on your project no larger than that. In other words, if you have planned in flexibility that you can make up a two-week delay, make the average work package no more than 80 hours. Then you can focus on "Are you done yet?" and produce clear and accurate reports on the status of your project.

Research and Evaluation

Research is the first step in the project life cycle. It includes the process of reviewing the available data from previous similar projects (the historical information we discussed in Chapter 6) as well as any available data specific to the current project. Performing this activity makes the rest of the project work faster and easier. It eliminates reinventing activities that have already been tried and proven.

Evaluation of how things went and the creation of lessons learned after the project is completed are hugely valuable in improving future projects. Therefore, evaluation must be included somewhere in every WBS.

When a project is done, it may not really be done. There needs to be some technical transition of the project to those who will perform the ongoing management of the product of the project. This transition is often forgotten in project life cycles.

Tricks for Creating the WBS

 The best method to create a WBS is to use sticky notes with the team to break the project down (decompose the project) into smaller, more manageable pieces.

 The WBS is created with the team, but it may also be done with other stakeholders or the sponsor present. This trick is especially helpful if the sponsor does not understand the work that needs to be done, or thinks it will take only a short amount of time. Having the sponsor present (but not contributing) during the WBS creation will help explain, in detail, why a project will take longer than the sponsor or stakeholders desire.

 Though the entire project team may not be identified at this stage, it is best to create a WBS with as close as possible to the final team, as a group. At a minimum, this improves buy-in and project quality, and decreases project risk.

 The project manager should create the top levels of the WBS before meeting with the team. It will give the team direction, let them see what a WBS is, and prevent wasted efforts.

 Add only work that is needed to complete the project deliverables. Do not include extra activities.

 To break each level down further, ask "What work do we need to do for this item in the WBS?"

Keep in mind that each level of the WBS is a smaller segment of the level above, and that the entire project is the aggregation of the highest levels of the WBS.

All of the work should be included in the WBS. If it is not in the WBS, it is not part of the project.

You will see that team members, managers, sponsors—everyone—gets really excited when they see a work breakdown structure or they help create one.

From a project manager's point of view, you get a chance to double check: Are you on the right track? Do you understand what is expected of you? Does the team understand what it will take to accomplish the work of the project?

Enabling Future Use of the WBS as Historical Information

When the WBS is completed, code numbers are assigned to help facilitate tracking of each work package later in the project, and in historical records long after the project is complete. This numbering scheme is also part of the WBS dictionary, covered later in this chapter. There are many different numbering schemes one can use, but generally they look like this:

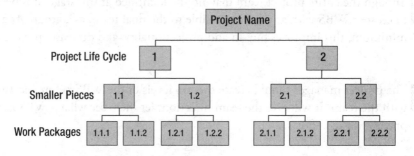

Business Value of the WBS

Estimates for a project at the smallest (work package) level improve accuracy. This is a key benefit of the WBS—the level of detail helps in creating the estimates, as well as staffing the project and proving how many people are needed. Risks on the project (what can go right and wrong) are also identified by work package.

Additional business benefits to creating a WBS include:

- Forces you to think through all aspects of the project
- Helps prevent work from slipping through the cracks
- Helps stakeholders get their minds around the project, its complexity, requirements, and constraints

- Provides the team members with an understanding of where their pieces fit into the overall project management plan and gives them an indication of the impact of their work on other activities of the project, as well as the project as a whole
- Facilitates communication and cooperation between and among the project team and other stakeholders
- Helps manage and control scope changes
- Focuses the team on what needs to be done, resulting in higher quality and a project that is easier to manage
- Provides a basis for estimating staff, cost, and time
- Provides validated evidence of the need for staff, budget, and time
- Can be reused for other projects

A WBS is so valuable that it should be done even for the smallest project. To gain the full benefit from the WBS, consider employing the following activities:

- Involve the entire team in creating and approving the WBS
- Work to pull out the team's ideas during WBS creation
- Include all the work
- Obtain approvals or sign-offs of the WBS from the project stakeholders
- Publish and distribute the WBS

Common Problems with Creating a WBS

Difficulty with Breaking Down WBS Elements If you are new to using the WBS, it is possible you will run into difficulties breaking down some parts of the diagram. The most likely cause of that difficulty is lack of scope clarity. Take the opportunity to ask the stakeholders clarifying questions and obtain the information needed to proceed with the WBS. As you do this, realize that this problem is saving you large amounts of time and money that you would have had to spend if this problem was not uncovered until later.

The "Project" Is More Than One Project When developing the WBS, if the project team cannot determine the next actions in one branch until other activities are defined in a separate branch, there are most likely multiple projects rolled into one.

Too Much Detail in the Work Package Remember the 8/80 rule: each work package should generally include work that will take between 8 and 80 hours. This makes managing the project easier in the long run.

The WBS Is Not the Schedule The WBS work packages are used to develop the project schedule, but the WBS is not the schedule itself. The schedule is created in the time management process, by breaking down the work packages to the activity level. That process also includes application of dates and deadlines to the activities.

WBS Is Developed by Functional Area The WBS is project specific. Some projects cross all of an organization's functional areas, and others will only impact a particular department. A WBS should never be developed by business unit. This method wastes time, adds costs, replicates activities, and is a poor way to organize a project.

Throughout the Project

The WBS will continue to provide value throughout the life of the project. The WBS can be used any time the project manager needs to reevaluate the scope of the project. For example:

- When there is a scope change to the project
- To evaluate any impacts of other changes on scope
- As a way to control scope creep by reminding everyone what work is to be done
- As a communications tool
- To help new team members see their roles

The WBS may be changed and updated throughout the project, and can be used to help stakeholders understand how their pieces fit into the whole project. On very small projects, where a detailed schedule has not been created, work packages in a WBS could be crossed off to show progress.

 Contributed by: Rhonda N. Allen
Atlanta, GA

To minimize re-engineering, which often leads to many changes in the project and greatly affects the overall cost of the project, I like to play the "what-if" game during design review. I develop a WBS and a process flowchart for different phases of construction to identify any potential gaps in the plan. I then ask the designer to explain how the design would change if a complication arises in each activity. A clear understanding of the techniques and alternatives available reduces the number of changes in execution. This increases the owner's or sponsor's confidence in the expected product and lays the groundwork for successful negotiations, should change become necessary.

The WBS Dictionary

The WBS dictionary could possibly be better termed "work package description." Its function is to provide the person completing the work package with a description of the work included in the work package. In addition to the work package description, the dictionary also should include any types of control such as sign-offs needed, cost and time estimates for the work package, and the acceptance criteria for the package. Most electronic project management tools readily enable both the WBS and the numbering scheme, making development of the documents fast and easy.

It may seem like overkill to have a WBS dictionary for small projects, but even the smallest project can end up with dozens or even hundreds of work packages. In addition, the information included in the dictionary adds value to the historical records, enabling more accurate project estimates for similar projects.

Following is a WBS dictionary form illustrating the information that should be included. An explanation of each field in the form follows.

WBS Dictionary		
Work Package Name/#	Date of Update	Responsible Organization/ Individual
Work Package Description		
Work Package Product		
Acceptance Criteria (How to know if the work is acceptable)		
Deliverables		
Assumptions		
Resources Assigned		
Duration		
Schedule Milestones		
Cost		
Due Date		
Interdependencies	Before this work package	
Interdependencies	After this work package	
Approved by Project Manager		Date

Work Package Name and Number The number helps to keep track of work packages, mapping to the WBS numbering schematic discussed earlier. By taking advantage of the same high-level WBS structures, a seasoned project manager will be able to quickly tell from the number with what piece of the project the work package is associated.

Date of Update Work packages, like the rest of the project, can change over time. Document control and configuration management activities require the project manager to make sure everyone has the correct version of any project document. Putting a date on it can help.

Responsible Organization/Individual In order to have accountability, each work package should be assigned to one person on the project team who will own the work. That person might need to form a small team to complete the work package, but the project manager would only need to interact with the person assigned the work package.

Work Package Description This section of the dictionary is best created with the help of the person assigned the work package for many reasons:

- The project manager is not required to know how to do all the work on the project, just how to manage it. The responsible person can provide the details necessary to complete the activities of the work package.
- Quality is much improved when the person who knows how to do the work completes the description.
- Commitment to actually completing the work on time is greatly improved if the person doing the work creates the description of the work. The work package becomes his or her work package, rather than the project manager's work package.
- The project manager will get a chance to look for scope creep in the description of the work package. The description also helps prevent scope creep later, as the work package is being completed.

Work Package Product Describing the end result of the work package helps the project manager be assured that the complete scope of the work package will be done. The product description also helps decrease the possibility of scope creep.

Acceptance Criteria The person completing the work should review his or her own work to make sure it is acceptable before providing it to the project manager. Having measures of success for the work package determined in advance will save time and improve quality.

Assumptions Assumptions made and found later to be incorrect can change the entire design of the project. Therefore, it is wise to document any assumptions made for each work package so the project manager can review the assumptions to check validity later on in the project.

Milestone

A significant event or checkpoint within the project schedule

Resources Assigned The project manager might assign resources to assist the person completing the work package. These resources can be people, equipment, or supplies, and should be described in the WBS dictionary.

Duration When compiling the WBS dictionary, it is important to estimate duration and cost at the same time. The concept of duration will be described in more detail in Chapter 10.

Schedule Milestones The creation of milestones for the project is another way for the project manager to control the project and to know how the project is doing while the work is underway. If a milestone date is met, the project may be on track Depending on the project, it might be useful for the person completing a work package to know to which milestone the work package belongs

Cost Cost estimates need to be captured for comparison to actual costs. Accurate cost estimates for each project help project managers who use historical information to be increasingly more accurate in their pricing models. Cost estimating will be discussed further in Chapter 10.

Due Date Once the project management plan is completed, each work package will have a date by which it must be completed without delaying the project. Such a date is listed in the WBS dictionary in order to keep focus on the date and prevent delay.

Interdependencies It is helpful to know what work comes before and after the work package. Sometimes knowing this will prevent the work package from being delayed because the effect becomes more widely known by the project team.

Approved by the Project Manager Approval implies authorization. Without approval, there can be no control.

Throughout the Project

The WBS dictionary is used:

- As a level of control for the project (e.g., Is the work being done on a work package level as described in the WBS dictionary?)
- To determine if a requested change is within the scope of the project
- To prevent scope creep
- To increase understanding of what needs to be done
- To increase buy-in to what needs to be done
- To send to functional managers or resource owners to inform them about what work their people are doing for the project
- As a reporting tool from those assigned the work package to the project manager
- As the high-level basis for the scope of work for any work to be outsourced or contracted

In the real world of project management, scope creep and lack of buy-in are significant problems that can cost the project a huge amount of time, money, and headaches. Project management is about preventing problems rather than dealing with them. The WBS dictionary is a key tool in the fight to manage and control projects.

Keep in mind that each WBS dictionary should be created by or with the person responsible for the work package. This aids in the responsible person taking ownership of the work package. Therefore, the project manager's work may not take much more time than reviewing and approving each work package, looking for added scope or misunderstanding of scope, and making sure the estimates are reasonable.

It is important to note that the WBS dictionary may be iterated as new information becomes available.

Here are some tricks to making the WBS dictionary work for you.

 When approved, a final copy of each WBS dictionary is provided to those who will complete the work package work. As the work is being done, team members use the WBS and WBS dictionary to confirm the work they are assigned.

The WBS dictionary can also form the basis for any work package level reporting. For example, team member status reports can be formatted to answer the questions of how they are doing in meeting deliverables, cost and time estimates, and acceptance criteria.

 If you think you will not have enough time, why not use this trick—just create WBS dictionaries for higher levels in the WBS rather than the work package level. This will create larger pieces, but still provide some level of control and buy-in.

Team Members

Team members can be involved in the work breakdown structure and WBS dictionary. They may:

- Help to break the first level of the WBS down to work packages
- Create, or assist the project manager in creating, WBS dictionaries for work assigned to them

Chapter Summary
Key Concepts
A WBS is:

- A hierarchical way to break a project into smaller, more manageable components or work packages
- A major precursor to budgeting, scheduling, communicating, allocating responsibility, and controlling the project

The business value of using a WBS:

- Improves the accuracy of project estimates
- Helps prevent work from slipping through the cracks
- Provides the team members with an understanding of where their pieces fit into the overall project management plan
- Facilitates communication and cooperation between and among the project team and other stakeholders
- Helps prevent scope changes
- Focuses the team on what needs to be done, resulting in higher quality and a project that is easier to manage

The business value of using a WBS dictionary:

- Provides a description of the work package product
- Provides information needed to control the work
- Provides an accurate and precise scope definition, thereby preventing scope creep

Questions for Discussion

How do the WBS and WBS dictionary help the project manager? How do they help the team?

Why should project management activities be included in the WBS?

Action Plan

1. What will you do differently in your real-world project management as a result of reading this chapter?
2. Add new items to your personal Tricks list in Chapter 2.

What Action?	Why?	By When?	Who Will Be Involved?	Who Will Be Affected?	Status

Goals of This Chapter

Upon completion of this chapter, you should be able to:

- Identify challenges in accurately estimating time and cost

- Articulate the value of accurate estimates

- Identify numerous techniques to improve estimating

- Explain three-point estimating

- Explain Monte Carlo analysis

Estimating project requirements is a science. Accurate estimates are important because they are a key metric in determining if the project was a success.

Many project managers create time and cost estimates without much support for the process, primarily because the estimates they have created in the past have been so unreliable. This chapter will help you prevent such problems.

First, take the time to describe specific difficulties you have seen in the real world with estimates.

Real-World Problems with Estimating on Projects

When you are finished, go to the free Web site (www.rmcproject.com/IT) and submit your list. You will then get a chance to see other's lists. Imagine the value of seeing the problems others have faced, so you might avoid the same problems on your own projects!

Estimating is not an isolated activity in project management. The groundwork that has been completed prior to asking for estimates will directly affect the quality of the estimates.

Consider the following list of common problems with estimates. Think about the tools and techniques we have discussed in this book that could prevent those problems. Apply what you have learned while completing this exercise.

Exercise:

Problem	How to Prevent It
Excessive padding—estimates that are intentionally too high	
Not all of the work is included in the estimates	
Misunderstanding of the actual work to be done	
Estimates are created by the wrong people	
Estimates change for no obvious reason	
Actual time or cost are significantly different than their estimates	

Answer:

Problem	How to Prevent It
Excessive padding—estimates that are intentionally too high	• Clearly define work packages in the WBS dictionary • Ask for the team members' opinions and involve them in estimating from the beginning so there is better trust • Explain to the team that padded estimates result in a schedule that they cannot rely on
Not all of the work is included in the estimates	• Make sure the WBS is complete • Make sure there is an estimate for each work package in the WBS
Misunderstanding of the actual work to be done	• Make sure the team member responsible for the work is involved in creation of the WBS dictionary • Make sure work packages are clearly defined in the WBS dictionary
Estimates are created by the wrong people	• Make sure the team member responsible for the work package is involved in estimating it
Estimates change for no obvious reason	• Do not allow estimates to be changed without a reason or without control of the project manager
Actual time or cost are significantly different than their estimates	• Use historical estimates as a sanity check • Make sure the team member responsible for the work package is involved in creating the WBS dictionary • Use three-point estimating • Reestimate during the project • Include the topic of estimating in a team meeting

There are numerous correct answers that address the issues with project estimating. The proper use of the WBS and WBS dictionary will help to avoid many of the problems associated with estimating. Problems with poor estimates are often directly related to the lack of a project management process, not an inability to estimate!

When proper project management methodology is followed, more realistic estimates can be created. A project manager needs to engage with team members from the beginning of the process: gathering requirements and expectations all the way through creating the WBS and WBS dictionary, and beyond. In this manner, the team has the opportunity to be involved and become vested in the success of the project.

Teams that are involved in the development of the WBS and WBS dictionary have a precise idea of the work involved in meeting the objectives of the project. They are in the best position to provide more accurate estimates for the work packages.

Techniques for Improving Estimates

Proper project management methodology throughout the project contributes to good project estimates. We have discussed the importance of the project manager laying the foundation by first identifying the stakeholders and then developing the project scope statement, WBS, and WBS dictionary. If the right stakeholders have been identified, and have had input into these elements of project planning, the resulting estimates will be more accurate.

Techniques to more finely hone project estimates include:

- Have the estimates created by those who will do the work
- Estimate small pieces so that the overall project estimate will be more accurate
- Remove the need to pad the estimate by providing or requesting the creation of a detailed description of the work to be estimated
- Have a connection between the work estimated and the cost, so as to better determine changes later; cost the scope at a detailed level
- Document the work to be estimated in detail in the WBS dictionary, and keep it in focus to prevent scope creep
- Make sure you understand effort (how long the work will take without interruption) and duration (over how long a time span the work will be completed)

- Record any assumptions
- Record variables and turn them into identified risks
- Communicate with those doing the estimating, letting them know how refined their estimates must be (e.g., ballpark or final)

Three-Point Estimating

You and the team members have done everything you can to describe the work. This does not guarantee that the team can determine an exact time or cost estimate. There are usually variables that need to be considered. The point is to not force the team members into hiding those variables from the project manager.

Instead of asking for a single estimate, the project manager might consider asking each team member who is providing estimates to instead provide three. The first would be the best case—everything goes our way. The second estimate would be the worst case scenario—everything that can go wrong does. The third estimate would be based on the team member's experience and perception of the most likely project rollout. This technique is called three-point estimating.

A three-point estimate is an estimate calculated based on the best case (optimistic), worst case (pessimistic), and most likely estimates for an activity, work package, or project.

Three-point estimating gives the project manager a better idea of the amount of variability in the estimates, and the team members do not need to pad their estimates. Knowing the level of variability in the estimates opens the door for the project manager and the team to utilize risk management techniques, described later in this book, to help further remove some of the causes of variability. The process of removing some or most of the variability in the estimates improves the quality of the estimates and thereby the overall project schedule and budget.

Value of the Three-Point Estimate

Once the project manager has the three-point estimates for each piece of work to be completed, the information can be used in different ways to help improve the project's estimates.

> **Three-Point Estimate**
>
> An estimate calculated based on the optimistic, pessimistic, and most likely estimates for an activity, work package, or project

121

- Use only the pessimistic estimates to create a project estimate. Using only the pessimistic values of the three-point estimates is the easiest solution for ensuring projects always come in on time and under budget. However, in this model, the stakeholders and management team will come to know the project manager as a "sandbagger" and hold any project analysis or project communications in low regard.
- Show management three project estimates (optimistic (O), pessimistic (P), and most likely (M)), so they are familiar with the range of possibilities. Calculate a weighted average by using the industry standard formula (O + 4M + P) divided by 6. This gives the stakeholders and management team a broader picture of how the project could unfold.
- Use software to perform a Monte Carlo analysis. Monte Carlo analysis can simulate the outcome of the project by making use of the three-point estimates to determine the probability of completing a project on a specific day at a specific cost.

Monte Carlo Analysis

Monte Carlo analysis can be accomplished using generally available spreadsheet software. The value of Monte Carlo analysis is in its ability to provide iterative evaluations of data using sets of numeric inputs. By changing the inputs, the project manager is able to graphically model the most accurate estimations of project.

Monte Carlo analysis is used when the model is complex and involves many uncertain parameters, as is found in project management estimation. It is used for analyzing uncertainty by measuring how input variations can affect the performance and reliability of the project being modeled.

The inputs for Monte Carlo are randomly generated from the probability distribution to simulate the process of samplings from an actual population. In our case, this means the random samples would be taken from the spectrum of the optimistic and pessimistic three-point analysis values. Monte Carlo analysis is capable of simulating the entire project hundreds of times, taking randomly selected values from each variable source each time. The output is a probability distribution of the overall resource estimates for the project as determined by the large numbers of iterations. This is why it is extremely important to have the best person available providing the work package estimates.

A Monte Carlo simulation might produce a diagram that looks like this:

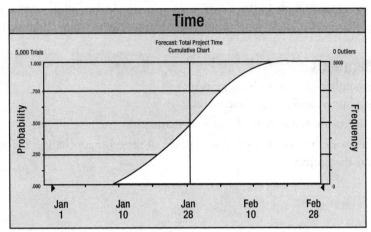

Throughout the Project

A project manager should continually look for indications that time and cost estimates need to be revised or might be erroneous. If the actual time or cost for one work package differs greatly from its estimate, a project manager should investigate all the estimates for similar work, and the other estimates from the same estimator.

On projects with long timelines, the project manager could reestimate all future work to double check the accuracy of estimates against current information. Or he or she could do a few random spot checks on similar work and other inputs from the estimator, if in a time crunch.

Major deviations in time or cost, missing a schedule milestone, or major risks occurring that were not identified are all indications that the entire project may be at risk and needs to be reestimated.

Estimates that are off for time or cost will result in changes to the other project constraints.

Time estimates and the WBS dictionary are used to formulate the project's schedule. Cost estimates are used to formulate the project's budget.

Creating a budget is generally a straightforward effort; adding up the cost estimates and adding contingency reserves for risk. Therefore, it is not covered as a separate chapter in this book. Keep in mind that a good budget will break down costs by work package, and will be usable to track total costs throughout the life of the project. Some budgets may include indirect costs such as overhead, but all should include contingency reserves. Contingency reserves are further discussed in Chapter 13.

Team Members

The team members' role in estimating is to:

- Provide honest and truthful estimates
- Work in collaboration with the project manager
- Let the project manager know if any aspect of the estimate changes before it impacts the project

Chapter Summary

Real-world estimating:

- Is dependent on work done previously in project planning, particularly the WBS and WBS dictionary
- Should be done by those doing the work
- May need to be revised later in the project

Three-point estimating:

- Provides an optimistic, pessimistic, and most likely outcome spectrum of estimates
- Is used as the input data for Monte Carlo analysis

Monte Carlo analysis:

- Is used for analyzing uncertainty
- Provides iterative evaluations of project estimating data inputs

Questions for Discussion

How can a project manager prevent padding in project estimates?

| |
| |
| |
| |
| |

What are the benefits of three-point estimating?

How is risk management related to estimating?

Action Plan

1. What will you do differently in your real-world project management as a result of reading this chapter?
2. Add new items to your personal Tricks list in Chapter 2.

What Action?	Why?	By When?	Who Will Be Involved?	Who Will Be Affected?	Status

Goals of This Chapter

Upon completion of this chapter, you should be able to:

- Explain the importance of scheduling and process flow

- Define the function of a project schedule

- Be able to read and understand a project management network diagram

- Define what a critical path is and how to use it to adjust the project to meet the required delivery date

TRICKS OF THE TRADE When assigning a project, it is not unusual for management to ask for a schedule, or to inquire as to how long you think the project will take to complete. However, there is much work that needs to be accomplished before even a preliminary project schedule can be developed. This is the opportune time to give a thumbnail rundown on the project management process and the importance of following the process flows.

The project management planning process flow is an optimized step-by-step order in which planning activities need to be accomplished. Process flows are used in every area of business. A good process flow ensures the maximum amount of work gets completed in the shortest amount of time. Process flows also take into account dependencies of other work activities needing to be completed to support the next step in the process.

Business executives understand the importance of process. However, they may need your help to understand the value of the project management process, and how it aligns with the achievement of their business objectives. Show them how allowing time to complete the project planning process will enable you to provide them with more accurate time and budget estimates.

Schedule development occurs after the creation of the WBS, WBS dictionary, activity list, and network diagram. The project schedule adds dates and times to the activities necessary to complete the project. The schedule enables the project manager to monitor work progress and avoid unexpected schedule slippages.

Project Management Software

Project management software is available in a variety of delivery models including desktop and enterprise licensed, hosted from a third party, or on a per-user-basis in the cloud. Project management software provides similar functionality across the vendors as well as the application delivery models. The software is used predominantly to create a schedule, graphically model the dependencies, support reporting functionality, and in many applications, what-if analysis. Many software vendors also provide elementary templates and forms that can be customized.

For information on considerations in selecting project software, please see Appendix B.

"Project management software" programs do not document all of the project management work that should be done, or all the forms that might be created. It is still up to the project manager to perform the work as described earlier in Rita's Process Chart and throughout this book. Software cannot be relied upon to do such things as requirements gathering and risk analysis that only a seasoned project manager can provide. Software applications cannot apply intelligence or business analytics to the inputs; that is the role of the project manager.

Most project managers use some form of software to create a schedule. This can be as simple as using spreadsheet software and basic symbols to show when work will be done, or as involved as the scheduling tool available in project management applications. Whether your scheduling technique is graphing paper and colored pencils or sophisticated software, this chapter will provide you with some tricks for creating a realistic schedule from the data already acquired in the project management planning process.

To create and work from an electronic schedule:

STEP 1. Enter the following information into your project management application:
- Project start date
- Work packages or smaller components, called activities, derived from the WBS

► Resource names for each activity (or skills for larger projects)

► Time to completion estimate for each activity; the activity duration

► Predecessor or dependency for each activity—what activity or activities must be done before this one can start

Based on these inputs, the application will produce a project management network diagram and a schedule. The network diagram shows which activities are dependent on others and how the project will flow from beginning to end.

The network diagram below illustrates a simple project flow.

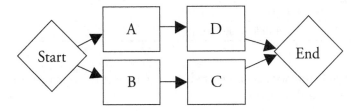

According to the network diagram, the activity represented by C will be completed only after activity B has been completed. Activity B is a predecessor of activity C. Put another way, activity C is dependent on the completion of activity B before it can begin; this is a finish-start relationship. Can you see how the network diagram helps get the project organized? Everyone can see how the work will flow from beginning to end.

In addition to graphically illustrating flow dependencies, the network diagram also shows what activities can be performed concurrently. In the above example, activities A and B can be performed at the same time. Once these activities are completed, activities D and C can be performed. Activities A and B do not have to end at the same time, and activities D and C are not required to begin at the same time. The diagram only shows that the activities can be conducted concurrently instead of sequentially.

Project management software can also take the dependency data and start dates and produce an initial schedule, called the schedule model, as shown in the following figure. This is the basic schedule you will work from and refine into the final schedule.

Network Diagram

(In project management terminology) Shows which activities are dependent on others, and how the project will flow from beginning to end

Project Schedule

A timeline to be followed for delivering the project's requirements and end product.

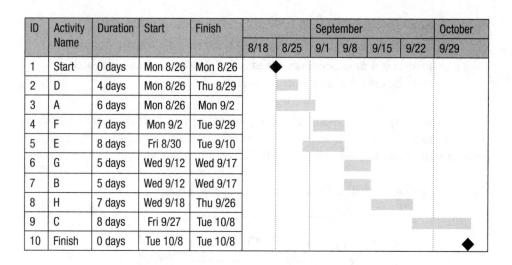

ID	Activity Name	Duration	Start	Finish		8/18	8/25	September	9/8	9/15	9/22	October
								9/1				9/29
1	Start	0 days	Mon 8/26	Mon 8/26								
2	D	4 days	Mon 8/26	Thu 8/29								
3	A	6 days	Mon 8/26	Mon 9/2								
4	F	7 days	Mon 9/2	Tue 9/29								
5	E	8 days	Fri 8/30	Tue 9/10								
6	G	5 days	Wed 9/12	Wed 9/17								
7	B	5 days	Wed 9/12	Wed 9/17								
8	H	7 days	Wed 9/18	Thu 9/26								
9	C	8 days	Fri 9/27	Tue 10/8								
10	Finish	0 days	Tue 10/8	Tue 10/8								

After the WBS dictionary data is entered into the project management tool, the project manager needs to then:

Step 2. Compare the end date that the software shows to the end date requested.

Step 3. If the electronically generated date falls within the range requested by management, add milestones to the schedule as a way for the project manager to control and confirm progress on the project.

Step 4. If the end date does not fall within the requested range, look for options to change the schedule by working with the project's critical path—the longest duration path through the schedule that accomplishes the project in the shortest time. Some options that may help in meeting the project delivery deadline include:

▶ Reduce risks on the project (see Chapter 13)

▶ Change the scope so that it takes less time

▶ Have more work done in parallel so the project gets completed faster (this is known as fast tracking the project schedule)

▶ Add resources to the project (this is a way of crashing the project schedule)

Step 5. Present the options to management and gain approval, or inform management that the required date cannot be reached based on the activities needed to be performed and provide a proposed alternative date.

Critical Path

The longest duration path through a network diagram; it determines the shortest time to complete the project

Present Options

The project manager is ethically bound to not blindly accept the end date requested. Prior to beginning project executing, the project manager must confirm that the requested date can be met based on the analysis of the project requirements, projected schedule, and the resources provided. The results of the project schedule analysis need to be presented to management to obtain approval. If there is any delta in the delivery date, either earlier or later than requested, the project manager needs to let management know what it will take to meet the desired end dates. These are not optional activities, but fundamental to project management.

When a project is authorized, there is usually a decision made by management regarding how much the project is worth to the company (measured in resources, cost, or time). When project management methodologies are not used to properly plan a project, there is a danger that the project will use more company resources than it should, based on its value or benefit to the company. This is one of the reasons projects are cancelled before they are completed.

The length of time the project will take needs to be determined before any work on completing deliverables begins. Any difference between estimated and desired dates must be reconciled. One of the key functions of a project manager is to "make it happen." The science of project management provides the project manager with the tools needed to determine options to accomplish the end output. The project manager must be able to come to management and not just report that the requested date can or cannot be met, but also provide options about what it will take to make it happen.

Putting this in action, a project manager might say, "You want the project completed within six months. We have analyzed the stakeholders' requirements, and developed a network diagram and schedule. The analysis shows that the minimum amount of time for this project, using current resources, will take nine months to complete. However, using project management techniques, our analysis indicates that if we delete requirement B from the IT department and requirement X from the Engineering department and add one more programmer to the team, we will then be able to meet the six-month date. Can you work with me to get these changes approved, or would you like to plan the project to take nine months?"

This phrasing, along with the WBS, network diagram, and preliminary schedule provides management with ample information to make informed decisions, rather than just being told it can or cannot be done. Even more importantly, it prevents a project from being started that cannot meet its end date. This is an example of where management can be involved and support the project in a beneficial manner. Note how productive such actions are, as opposed to making the six-month schedule happen and letting the IT and Engineering departments find out at the last minute that their requirements are not included in the project.

What-if Analysis

The determination of what activities can be accomplished to meet a desired end date.

The essence of scheduling is not the use of software, but the application of what-if analysis—the determination of what can be done to meet a desired end date. Scheduling is proactive. With so many options to decrease the schedule, having an unrealistic schedule just shows a lack of proper application of project management methodology. An unrealistic schedule is the project manager's fault.

 Giving team members a chance to approve the final schedule helps increase buy-in to the schedule and uncover any items the project manager might have missed.

Exercise:

Exercise Data: Your project planning so far has resulted in estimates and a network diagram as shown below:

Activity	Predecessor	Duration in Weeks
Start	None	0
A	Start	4
B	A	2
C	B	10
D	A	15
E	C	16
F	C	16
G	C	15
H	F	6
I	G	9
J	H, I	1
K	D, J, E	6

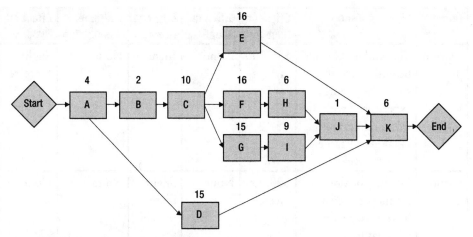

There are four paths through this network:

Start, A, D, K, END totaling 25 weeks
Start, A, B, C, E, K, END totaling 38 weeks
Start, A, B, C, F, H, J, K, END totaling 45 weeks
Start, A, B, C, G, I, J, K, END totaling 47 weeks

The Question: Based on the previous information, the longest or critical path is Start, A, B, C, G, I, J, K, END. This path has a duration of 47 weeks. However, management has stated that the project must be completed in 43 weeks. Based on the following options, which would you select to meet management's requirements and save 4 weeks?

Option	Effect on Time	Effect on Cost	Effect on Scope	Effect on Quality	Customer Satisfaction	Effect on Risk
Option 1	Part of the scope for D could be cut, resulting in D taking 12 instead of 15 weeks.	$20,000 savings	Decrease	None	Huge decrease	Slight decrease
Option 2	E could be done after B rather than C.	None	None	None	None	Huge increase

Option	Effect on Time	Effect on Cost	Effect on Scope	Effect on Quality	Customer Satisfaction	Effect on Risk
Option 3	The work in G could be outsourced to a company more experienced with the work, resulting in G taking 11 rather than 15 weeks.	$30,000 savings	None	Increase	None	Slight Increase
Option 4	H could be done by another person in your company who has more experience. This would change its duration from 6 to 4 weeks.	$28,000 increase	None	Slight increase possible	None	None
Option 5	The work in F could be completed a different way than currently planned, using older technology but still meeting requirements. F would then take 14 rather than 16 weeks.	$4,000 savings	Change	None	None	Decrease

Indicate your option choice and explain why you selected that particular option.

Answer:

Options 1 and 2 are not good choices because they are not on the critical path. These options would have no impact on the duration of the critical path, and so would not give you the time savings needed.

Option 3 seems to be the best option until you realize that it really only saves 2 weeks. Although the duration of activity G changes from 15 to 11 weeks, resulting in a decrease of 4 weeks, such a decrease on this path makes another path the longest one. The change to activity G makes path Start, A, B, C, F, H, J, K, End, with a duration of 45 weeks, the longest or critical path. So, this option changes the project length from 47 to 45 weeks. This is a good first step, but it does not save us enough time. We need to keep looking.

At first glance, options 4 and 5 do not deal with the critical path and so do not look like good choices. However, remember that because we have selected option 3, we are now dealing with a new critical path (Start, A, B, C, F, H, J, K, End). Selecting option 3 made the critical path duration 45 weeks. We need to get it to 43 weeks by saving at least two more weeks. Options 4 and 5 now affect the critical path. Let's see if either option is a good choice when combined with option 3.

Option 4 saves 2 weeks on the new critical path, but it has a $28,000 cost increase. Why increase cost if we do not have to?

Option 5 saves 2 weeks on the new critical path and also saves $4,000 and results in decreased risk.

As a result, the best choice is a combination of options 3 and 5.

 Contributed by: Kathy Phillips
Winchester, MA

I use this trick on projects where the target date has been mandated (either by law or by management fiat) and the team has to "back into" the project plan. It has proven very useful in both getting business buy-in and educating partners on project management levers.

My trick is to illustrate the constraints imposed using the actual project timeline as opposed to an ideal project timeline (where the date is not imposed). I begin by stating that the scope, timeline, and resources have been established, and that the only lever the team has in meeting the date is quality. I then overlay the actual and ideal timelines on a chart and show two points on the timescale: where we would anticipate all defects to be identified and where we would expect to have them all fixed. For example, the project might have an ideal timeline where testing runs four months—say, from January to April—but the actual timeline is only two months. Ideally, we would have completed testing and identified defects by mid-March and fixed defects by mid-April. In the real world, we won't have even identified them all, never mind fixed them.

We work closely with business partners to prioritize defects and build workarounds for each. The business then determines if they are willing to "go live," given the total number of workarounds they will need to implement. This creates a partnership and makes joint ownership of the result clear. It also assures that the business is truly prepared, that expectations are managed, and that a post-implementation work queue is identified and prioritized.

Throughout the Project

Smart project managers will realize that a schedule is only an estimate. As we discussed in Chapter 10, the schedule may need to be recompiled during the project to make sure end dates can be met. Then, when the schedule is approved, the project manager must ensure the project is kept on track to meet the schedule date and associated milestones.

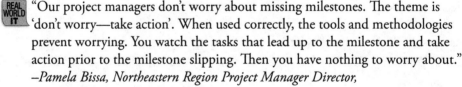 "Our project managers don't worry about missing milestones. The theme is 'don't worry—take action'. When used correctly, the tools and methodologies prevent worrying. You watch the tasks that lead up to the milestone and take action prior to the milestone slipping. Then you have nothing to worry about."
—Pamela Bissa, Northeastern Region Project Manager Director,
SunGard Higher Education
Read the complete interview with Pamela Bissa in Appendix C.

Following are some tricks to help you with schedule management.

TRICKS OF THE TRADE Remember that your project management activities should include more than just managing the schedule. People new to project management often make the mistake of spending all of their time managing the schedule, when other activities discussed in this book, such as dealing with the prevention of problems, would have a greater impact. That said, you still need to manage the schedule.

TRICKS OF THE TRADE Make sure everyone involved with the project, including stakeholders, the sponsor, and the project team, knows what the current schedule is. Highlight the person's name, or put a handwritten message on the schedule, so the schedule is noticed when it is received by each individual.

TRICKS OF THE TRADE Look for significant changes in work package due dates that result from schedule updates, and make sure those doing the work packages are aware of the new dates.

TRICKS OF THE TRADE Send copies of the project schedule to team members' bosses to make sure they are aware of how much time is required from each human resource, and when that resource will be returned. This helps the bosses plan their work loads, reducing the potential of a resource being redeployed to other activities unexpectedly.

TRICKS OF THE TRADE Look for the need and the opportunity to move resources around as a result of changes in the schedule.

Contributed by: Mary M. Bagley
Williamsville, NY

By the end of business on Thursdays, I send out an e-mail to all key team members and sponsors giving an update on the project. The format is as follows:

Hello Everybody:
We are nearly complete on our project and have X weeks until go-live. We are where we planned to be/behind/ahead of schedule at this time. Thanks to everyone for our success so far!

Attached are the status report, calendar, and high-level project schedule for the XXXX Project.

I also attached a vacation calendar for your review. Please let me know of your vacation plans.

Team Members

Project managers create the schedule. Team members' involvement may include:

- Confirm that the calendar dates that result from their estimates are acceptable
- Help to determine options for shortening the schedule
- Support the project manager's efforts to meet with management and avoid an unrealistic schedule

Chapter Summary
Key Concepts
A realistic project schedule:

- Is dependent on the accuracy of work done earlier in the project (project scope statement, WBS, estimates)
- Must be determined before the project executing process starts
- May be created with the help of project management software
- Directly relates to the other project constraints
- May need to be adjusted during the project

Projects should never be started without an approved schedule.

Project managers have an obligation to do all of the project planning work, including developing the schedule, prior to accepting or declining a required delivery date.

Project managers have electronic tools available to perform what-if analysis that aids in determining viable alternatives for meeting a required project delivery date.

Questions for Discussion
Define the following terms: project schedule, critical path, and what-if analysis.

How does knowing the critical path help the project manager?

What value does what-if analysis provide a project manager?

What are some of the project manager's options when faced with a required end date that cannot be met?

Action Plan

1. What will you do differently in your real-world project management as a result of reading this chapter?
2. Add new items to your personal Tricks list in Chapter 2.

What Action?	Why?	By When?	Who Will Be Involved?	Who Will Be Affected?	Status

Communications Management

Goals of This Chapter

Upon completion of this chapter, you should be able to:

- Develop a communications management plan

- Identify the elements that make up the communications management plan

- List areas of a project that need to be communicated regularly, and to whom

- List the best ways to communicate specific types of information

Effective communication can be difficult, especially when you deal with team members you have not met, and/or when team members are from different cultures. When you add bad communication habits and methods to the mix, communication problems on IT projects only become compounded.

How many times have you listened to a voicemail message and deleted it before the message was over? How many times have you looked at the beginning of an e-mail, thought it was not relevant, and read no more, only to find out later that there was important information at the end? Have you ever engaged in an e-mail exchange where the subject line no longer supports the content? Such actions contribute to ineffective communication. These are not small problems, and the key to solving them starts with eliminating these behaviors in yourself and your team.

Ineffective communication is one of the leading problems a project manager has on a project. A project manager spends most of his or her time communicating. As you read through the interviews in Appendix C, you will notice that no matter how large or small the company, how new or seasoned they are to project management tools and methodologies, effective communication reaps significant benefits for the project, the company, and the customer. A communications management plan must be created during the project planning process.

A communications management plan is crucial for IT projects. As the interviewees discuss in Appendix C, workgroup and department requirements change. The group lead may not even consider how seemingly small changes within the workgroup will impact the ability to integrate the output of the project with the revised workgroup strategy.

Consider the following example of how one workgroup technology change can have a ripple effect throughout the entire IT organization. Your team is working on a project that involves integrating all of a workgroup's communication systems. This project includes bringing together the desktop instant messaging and presence clients, the IP-based telephone, and establishing a standard for mobile smart devices for the company. The objective of your project is for the members of the workgroup to be able to obtain and respond to all e-mail and voicemail in real time, whether they are in the office or working remotely.

The company has standardized its IT infrastructure to optimize applications and throughput efficiencies. Your team is working merrily along, integrating the Microsoft IM and presence clients and the softphone with the back-end voice message store. It has negotiated a terrific deal on smart phones and data access support with the mobile carrier. Just as you are about to roll out the solution and start training, you learn the workgroup has gone off and purchased netbooks. Well, that certainly creates a dilemma for your project's ability to be successful. Had you been communicating regularly with the group lead, you would have learned they were planning to move their team's applications into the cloud, the virtual environment. Now, not only do you have a failed project on your hands, but you also have a workgroup leader who has established a different paradigm for workgroup activities. What a mess.

Effective Project Communication

Is detailed and clearly specified in the communications management plan as part of the project management plan

The secret to effective communication is to recognize that the communication methods must be detailed and clearly specified in the communications management plan. A project manager cannot rely on random or ad hoc communication for a project to be successful.

The first steps toward quality communication have already been taken. Early in the project management process, all of the stakeholders have been identified, stakeholder requirements and expectations have been determined, and the scope has been finalized as much as possible. These basic project management actions have eliminated many communication problems, because the project's scope and requirements have been defined.

Formal communications planning occurs next. The communications management plan identifies what needs to be communicated on the project, to whom, when, by what method, and how frequently. The communications management plan should include analysis and accomodation of the stakeholders' communications requirements. The plan also includes specific strategies and methods for communicating with the internal team as well as with the customer or client.

Effective communication goes beyond writing weekly status reports. An effective project manager seeks to continually monitor the project's expected output with the current stakeholders' situations. Had our project manager in the preceding scenario been in regular dialogue with the workgroup leader, the project could have been modified to accommodate the new paradigm, or the project could have been shelved without wasting any further time and money. It is nearly impossible for a project manager to over-communicate.

Exercise:

What do you think needs to be communicated on a project to the internal stakeholders?

Answer:

A basic list should include:

- Status
- Project charter
- Project management plan
- WBS
- When resources will be needed
- Meeting schedule
- Work assignments
- New risks uncovered
- Problems
- Changes
- Updates to components of the project management plan
- Upcoming work
- Delays
- Performance

 More advanced project managers will also be concerned with communicating the following:

- Success
- Achievement
- Confidence
- What is worrying team members
- Parts of the project management plan about which team members are unsure
- The date of the next milestone completion party
- Changes to project or product scope
- Impacts of changes on project or product scope
- Impacts between this project and other projects

To be effective, communications must include communicating in all of the following directions and with the following types of people:

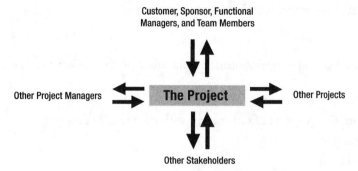

Communication is a two-way street. The project manager must continually seek to obtain information even as he or she sends information out. Effective communication is more than sending or acquiring information. As identified in all of the interviews in Appendix C, exceptional project managers share with the executive sponsor and internal stakeholders their confidence in their ability to handle the project, seeking their assistance before problems get out of control.

Review the earlier lists of what needs to be communicated. Can you think of more items that might need to be communicated over the life of the project?

TRICKS OF THE TRADE: What needs to be communicated from the project manager to others associated with the project?

- Updates on resources needed, and when
- Changes to the project, and their impacts on the project and product
- Issue log items from meetings
- That the project manager cares about and is committed to a successful outcome for the project
- The project manager's integrity
- That the project manager is in control of the project
- That the project manager is open to hearing conflicting ideas, problems, and new ideas from stakeholders
- Status of specific requirements
- Schedule for interactions with other departments
- The best way to get information to the project manager

- The best way to find out information about the project
- Discoveries and lessons learned
- Assignments and due dates for upcoming work

 What needs to be communicated from others to the project manager?

- Level of commitment
- Happiness or level of satisfaction with the project's progress
- Changes
- Problems
- Risks
- Achievement of milestones
- Areas of confusion
- Hidden agendas
- What they like and do not like about the project
- Areas where they could provide extra help to the project
- Frustrations
- Little things that could become bigger
- Things the project manager missed
- The project manager's performance, both positive and negative feedback
- How the project can be improved
- New ideas
- Discoveries
- Lessons learned

Recall from childhood Aesop's fable, *The Boy who Cried Wolf*. Every time the boy took his flock of sheep to graze, he would cry wolf and the community would come running to his aid, only to discover there wasn't a wolf. One day there actually was a wolf, but when the boy called out, no one came to his rescue and the wolf ate all the sheep.

As a project manager, communicating is similar to the fable. It is important to communicate regularly with the stakeholders involved in the project, yet not every message needs to be shared with every stakeholder. If you flood everyone's e-mail and voicemail boxes with every bit of project information, whether the information pertains to them or not, they will start deleting content without listening to or reading it. When you need assistance in clearing a hurdle, no one will know because they have been trained to ignore you.

As you read through the interviews in Appendix C, one item that bubbles up across all of them is the human factor. You are dealing with all sorts of personalities, egos, career-minded team members, and those seeking different careers. Your role is to bring a project to successful completion within the parameters of the project constraints. If you keep your end goal in mind, along with the fable, it becomes easier to see who needs what information.

For example, personality issues that interfere with the project's success need to be addressed between the parties involved, but not communicated to the entire team, the stakeholders, or the customer. Achievement of milestones should be widely communicated. As the project manager, if you need assistance in lining up resources for the next phase of the project, resources being requested and their managers need to be in the communication loop. If you are unsure if a particular party should be involved in a communication thread, ask them directly.

Another solution to the risk of communication overload is to set up a collaborative, social network site. The site holds all of the information pertaining to a specific project, allows team members to actively engage in conversations that are threaded by topic, and includes all of the project's documents and ongoing reports. A central repository, accessible by all of the stakeholders, allows people to do project status checks at their convenience. This is not to say the project manager is now free to stop communicating on a regular basis. The reports and updates absolutely need to be completed on a timely, regular basis. The central repository is simply a safety net to ensure all project-related documents are in a known location and accessible to those involved in the project's execution.

Communicating is not tricky, but it does need to be conducted with thoughtfulness and consideration of everyone's time and respective roles within the project.

The project manager creates a communications management plan with input from the team, executive sponsor, stakeholders, and customer. A very simple plan might look like this:

What Needs to be Communicated	Why	Between Whom	Best Method for Communicating	Responsibility for Sending	When and How Often

Everyone has a preferred method and style of communicating. Communication is also influenced by the company's culture. Communications may be formal, informal, written, or verbal, and may be accomplished using any or a combination of the following methods:

- E-mail
- Handwritten letter
- Face-to-face meeting
- Teleconference
- Phone call
- Personal conversation
- Overnight delivery
- Standardized report
- Project Web site
- Fax
- Video conference

Communications planning involves asking questions such as:

- Would it be better to communicate the information in an e-mail or telephone call?
- Is this an issue that I should go to see the person about?
- Should I send a letter through the mail in order for it to get real attention?

The process of communications planning forces us to think about the best way to communicate so that we do not send urgent communications by e-mail to someone who never looks at their e-mail; so we do not pick up the phone when we really need to meet with the person we need to communicate with. A major cause of communication problems is simply selecting the wrong method of communication.

A few rules of thumb will help you determine the optimal method to communicate.

- Bad news should be delivered face-to-face, time permitting.
- Urgent bad news, when the party is not available to meet, should be delivered over the phone, but not left in a voicemail.
- Good news should be delivered via e-mail for ease of sharing.
- Personal accolades should be delivered face-to-face, preferably in a team meeting.
- Accolades should also be put in writing and the person's direct manager cc'd.

In the communications management plan, make sure the following items are addressed:

- Responsibility charts—Who is accountable for what? Who should talk to whom?
- How will you interface with other organizations involved in the project?
- How will you interface with the stakeholders?
- What reporting form does the sponsor require?
- What reporting form do you want from the project team?
- How will you clearly delineate project roles and responsibilities?
- What methods should the team use to bring problems or issues to your attention?
- What are the problem escalation procedures?

Exercise:

Consider the following communication problems and develop strategies to address them.

Communication Problem	How to Prevent It
A team member did not know when his work needed to be done.	
An e-mail was not read in time to take appropriate action.	
The project manager cannot get management to help resolve a technical dispute.	
A team member says she told the project manager about a change to the WBS dictionary, but the project manager has no record of any such conversation.	

Potential Answers:

Communication Problem	How to Prevent It
A team member did not know when his work needed to be done.	Review the communications management plan to see if the team member received an updated copy of the schedule and if he understood how to interpret the schedule.
An e-mail was not read in time to take appropriate action.	Investigate how many e-mails the person receives and review the plan for handling e-mail on your project. Bring such issues up at the next team meeting.
The project manager cannot get management to help resolve a technical dispute.	Let management know how much time and cost the project will incur if the problem is not resolved.
A team member says she told the project manager about a change to the WBS dictionary, but the project manager has no record of any such conversation.	Ask the team member to show that the message was sent. Explain the impact to the project that the problem caused. Ask her for ideas of how to prevent it in the future.

Take a few minutes to complete another exercise. Make a list of communication problems you have faced on your projects, and then determine what you can do to prevent similar problems in the future.

Exercise:

Communication Problem	How to Prevent It

One of the biggest values to you in this chapter may be the ideas on our Web site. Add your problems and solutions to the list at www.rmcproject.com/IT and gain access to the responses of other project managers from around the world.

IN THE FIELD
Contributed by: Kerry R. Wills
Hartford, CT

Within project planning, I like to create a "community plan," where a one-page plan is created and then posted on everyone's desktop or a wall. This is a technique that can be used at most points in a project, but up-front is probably the most genuinely received and beneficial.

By contributing to the community plan, team members have ownership of the dates, rather than feeling as though the dates were given to them. People have a hard time committing to activities that they didn't help to plan.

Also, by seeing all of the activities and dates, the team can understand the context of their work and be reminded of when deliverables are due. This seems simple, but oftentimes the plan is hidden away and the team members don't even see it to know what the dates are, or the other activities happening within the project.

Like the town clock of ancient times, all of your "villagers" will be looking at the same clock, and all will know exactly what time it is.

 Contributed by: Tim Menke, PMP, Lean Sigma Black Belt
Rochester Hills, MI

I'm accustomed to managing technical projects staffed with engineers and software developers. I once had the opportunity to take over a struggling human resources project in support of a company merger.

The team of HR professionals reacted to my proposed recovery plan, a Microsoft Project Gantt chart, less than enthusiastically. I quickly realized that these folks didn't live in the world of predecessors, successors, float, slack, or even duration that was commonplace with my technical teams. My disappointment was obvious, but short-lived, as I noticed all of the team members had calendars and/or "to-do" lists in front of them.

I had my project scheduler rerun the same schedule using the calendar month view. I was amazed at how much differently the team reacted to the exact same information in a format that was more familiar and less intimidating to them. I subsequently had 30-60-90 day "look ahead" activity lists printed for each team member, so they could insert them in their planners.

Simply changing the format of the reports enabled me to get the team engaged in planning and executing the project, and provided me with the information I needed to maintain project control. The team members rarely saw the underlying Gantt chart from which their calendars and activity lists were generated, but it was there!

Throughout the Project

Communications planning does not end after the project is planned. It is important for the project manager to revisit the communications management plan and even to solicit comments and changes to the plan throughout the life of the project.

Communications require structure and careful thought. If communication is indeed the number one problem on projects, then thinking about managing good communication should be a primary focus of a project manager while the work is underway. Such activities might include using the following tricks:

 Take the time to ask key stakeholders to identify any aspects of the project they are unsure of, thereby preventing communication problems rather than just dealing with them.

 Update the communications management plan whenever problems or new communication-related needs are uncovered.

 To keep a focus on communication problems, add "recent communication problems" to the agenda for team meetings and have those who had the problems describe them and how they were resolved.

 Don't forget nonverbal communication. Sophisticated project managers know that a substantial amount of communication takes place through body language. Also consider tone of voice and word choice for communication clues.

Think outside the box! Here are some creative examples of ensuring good communication on projects.

 A project manager needed to make sure that someone received and read a report, but the person who was to receive the report was known for not reading them. What did the project manager do? He arranged for a man in a gorilla suit to deliver the report. Naturally, it got noticed!

A project manager had little experience in managing projects and was worried that there was something important that he did not learn while planning the project. Instead of worrying, he decided to hold a contest with a prize for the team member who informed the project manager about the biggest thing he did not know.

 A project team was loaded down with too many e-mails. Many problems were occurring because people did not get to their e-mail in time, even though they had agreed that this was the best method of communicating the issues. The project manager instituted a new rule that each e-mail should have a 1, 2, or 3 in the subject matter line; 1 for "read it right now," 2 for "read it within two days," and 3 for "I am not sure this affects you, but you should take a quick look at it."

 A project manager was managing a project that had few objective measures of success. She was concerned about how to determine how things were going. Instead of just holding regular team meetings, the project manager added a new feature. Every other time the team met, the project manager would ask them to rate on a 1 to 10 scale (10 being the highest) how confident they were that the project would be completed on time. She tracked the results and knew when to investigate further and when investigation was not necessary.

 A project manager, new to the company, was leading a project. In order to encourage team members to bring issues to him, he handed out pieces of paper to the team at a team meeting. He asked each person to name a hidden objective of the team member sitting to that person's right-hand side.

 Contributed by: Alan E. Feinberg
Rockville, MD

I managed a large multi-disciplined team that was dispersed among various locations. Keeping everyone informed about the program was a prime problem. I found that official e-mails, correspondence, status reports, program reviews, etc., were often ignored by various members of the team, or not fully distributed to all concerned. After I started an informal newsletter, which I e-mailed to all members of the project team, our internal communications greatly improved. Basically, my goal was to convey information without being too heavy about it. I tried to write this newsletter in the style of a "hometown rag," making references to classic rock songs, using colloquial language, and keeping it folksy, humorous, and down to earth. In addition to program highlights, status, and other essential management information, I kept the publication human by congratulating people on work and personal achievements, sending holiday and birthday greetings, and occasionally including recipes or silly stories. I included trivia on various arcane subjects, and even held contests. In fact, the first contest was to name the newsletter. I also solicited input from the readers on both professional and non-professional topics and included their contributions in later issues. After awhile, the publication became self-sustaining and virtually wrote itself. My ultimate validation was when I actually got requests from personnel working other programs to be included on our distribution list because it was so informative. Long story short, my newsletter became a must-read publication and was a valuable tool in promulgating information to my team and others in the organization.

 Contributed by: C. Poovannan
Hyderabad, Andhra Pradesh, India

When I e-mailed weekly progress reports as attachments to the stakeholders, most of them didn't open the attachments immediately. The result was that crucial information about the project didn't always reach them in a timely manner. In addition, the attachment of lengthy reports added an undue load to the exchange server.

I found the trick of converting the report to an HTML document and sending it directly in an e-mail to the stakeholders. This allowed them to easily access the information in the message itself, rather than in an attachment. Further, I added a column in the progress report which recognized the official/personal achievements of the stakeholders during that week. This was motivating for them, and everybody was happy to see their names reflected in the report, which was read by a large group of stakeholders.

We have experienced massive improvement in project communication using this approach, and this practice is now followed by most of my project management office colleagues in our company. Even the IS team is appreciative that the load on the exchange server has been drastically reduced.

Team Members

Team members' role in communications management can include:

- Let the project manager know what method or form of communication is best for them on the project
- Help to create the communications management plan for the project
- Follow the communications management plan
- Let the project manager know of communication issues that are not addressed in the communications management plan
- Let the project manager know of instances where the communications management plan was not helpful
- Work to make sure all their communications are clear and effective
- Keep communication issues at the forefront of their thoughts

Chapter Summary
Key Concepts
Communications:

- Must be planned into the project
- Must meet the needs of stakeholders
- Must involve the team so they take ownership
- Must be vigilantly monitored and measured for effectiveness

Questions for Discussion
Why is it important to have a formal communications management plan?

What things are likely to be forgotten in communications planning?

How should a project manager manage communications throughout the life of the project?

Action Plan

1. What will you do differently in your real-world project management as a result of reading this chapter?
2. Add new items to your personal Tricks list in Chapter 2.

What Action?	Why?	By When?	Who Will Be Involved?	Who Will Be Affected?	Status

Preventing Problems: Identifying and Managing Risk

Goals of This Chapter

Upon completion of this chapter, you should be able to:

- Explain the process of risk management

- Define and explain how to establish reserves

- Develop a risk management plan as part of project planning

A project manager was excited to be working on one of the most important projects in the company. Partway through the project, a supplier to the project suffered a shutdown of one of their main facilities, thereby delaying shipment to many of their clients. That project manager was leaving work that day when one of his company's senior managers stopped him and said, "How can you be leaving work on time when we have such a major problem to deal with? Shouldn't you be holding some kind of troubleshooting meeting?" The project manager said, "No need; we already have a plan in place for just such an occurrence. No meeting is required. The shutdown will only affect our project slightly."

How good would you feel if you were this project manager? How exciting would project management be if every day was filled with scenarios like the one just described? This is what risk management is all about. As you read through the interviews in Appendix C, notice how each company addresses risk planning. Each interview subject noted that they fully expect situations to arise over the course of a project. However, being able to anticipate the risks, and having risk response plans in place allows the project managers to keep their projects on track.

The purpose of risk management is twofold. The first objective of risk management is to identify and eliminate as many potential threats to the project as possible; then to reduce the negative impact of the remaining threats on the project. The second objective is to identify as many potential opportunities as possible, and to plan the project in a manner that enables the company to take advantage of these opportunities.

Risks

Events that can affect the project for better or worse

Opportunities or threats

When project managers use risk management, they have developed a contingency plan for what to do if a negative risk occurs on the project. There is also a fallback plan, should the contingency plan not work out. One of the objectives of project management is risk avoidance, but a project manager must always have a backup strategy to deal with the unavoidable risks.

Risks evolve and change over the life of the project. Notice in the P&G and the CH2M HILL interviews how these firms consistently return to the risk management plan at each milestone. Implementing their risk management plan allows them to evaluate risks on the project as well as to evaluate how the rollout of the project may be impacting other areas of the company that were not initially taken into consideration. Following the risk management plan over the course of the project mitigates potentially wider and broader problems across the company.

Within IT, there are many opportunities associated with using risk management on a project. For example, software or software applets developed on one project can be used with other clients and applications. Many IT projects are replicated across workgroups and departments. Understanding where the business process workflow of each intersects adds value to risk management plans by saving time and money on projects that involve interconnected workgroups. These are direct, measurable opportunities that reduce project time and cost on other projects.

Several of the interviews in Appendix C provide real-world examples of using risk management effectively. The ETG interview addresses the risk of a supplier not being able to fulfill its hardware orders, an example of a negative risk, by engaging with multiple equipment suppliers. In the Clikthrough interview, we learn that the company monitors and takes advantage of software development requests that can be broadly applied to its existing client base as well as its internal software assets, an example of opportunity.

The Process of Risk Management

Although the steps of the risk management process occur in sequence, it is important to remember that they are repeated throughout the project. Even when a risk is identified after the initial risk identification process, it must be analyzed, responses must be planned, etc. The risk management process is very iterative.

Risk Management Planning The project manager, with the sponsor, project team, customer, stakeholders, and experts determine how risk management will be done on the project, who will be involved, and procedures to be used.

Risk Identification Specific risks are identified for the project and for each work package or activity. This effort should involve all stakeholders and might even involve literature reviews, research, and talking to nonstakeholders. Sometimes the core team will begin the process and then the other members will become involved, making this an iterative process.

Qualitative Risk Analysis Using a standard scale such as Low, Medium, High, or 1 to 10, the project manager and team subjectively rate the probability and impact of each risk. Qualitative risk analysis enables the sorting and prioritization of a project's risk list.

Quantitative Risk Analysis Numerical analysis of each risk's probability and impact (amount at stake or consequences), and analysis of how the risks could impact the accomplishment of the project objectives, is performed.

Risk Response Planning This process involves defining what can be done to reduce the overall risk on the project by decreasing the probability or impact of threats, and increasing the probability or impact of opportunities.

Risk Monitoring and Control The risk response plan is executed to manage the project's risks and control the overall project risk.

As a result of the risk management process, every risk is assigned to someone to manage; that person becomes the risk response owner. In the event a risk occurs during the project, the risk response owner is able to take immediate action to leverage or thwart the risk, depending on its nature.

When risk management is done on a project, the project manager is able to spend his or her time implementing contingency plans and fallback plans rather than holding meetings to determine what actions to take. The project manager is proactive and in control of the project.

 How do you know when you have identified enough risks? Do it until it becomes silly. This might seem like an ineffective trick until you try it. To be really effective, risk identification should involve the identification of possibly hundreds of risks, not just five or ten.

 Lists of risks are part of every project's historical file. (See Chapter 6.) After completing the risk identification process, project managers should review the historical files of similar projects for more ideas of potential threats or opportunities.

IN THE FIELD *Contributed by: Ed Delker, PMP*
Wentzville, MO

Sometimes major stakeholders are less than forthcoming in discussing key business drivers and risks. After setting the stage with a series of open-ended questions about the project from the stakeholder's perspective, if I am getting minimal elaboration from the stakeholder, I'll ask the person, "What kind of things will get you fired?" Or, I might ask what will get their boss fired. The questions have a certain amount of shock value, but they definitely get a stakeholder focused on the personal consequences of not managing risk. This invariably leads to identification and prioritization of risks that may not come out of polite conversation.

Risk Register

One document for the entire risk management process that will be constantly updated with information as the risk management processes are completed

Included in historical records that will be used for future projects

Developing and Using the Risk Register

The risk register is the output of the risk planning process. It documents all of the identified risks, contingency plans, and fallback plans for each risk, and the risk owners assigned. The risk register becomes part of project's historical information file.

13 CHAPTER

Exercise:

Risk Register for _____ (Insert project name)				
Things That Can Go Right (Opportunities)				
Risk	P	I	P x I	Response Plan
Things That Can Go Wrong (Threats)				
Risk	P	I	P x I	Response Plan

P = Probability   I = Impact

To see examples of project risks from project managers around the world, visit the RMC Web site at www.rmcproject.com/IT.

Not all risks carry the same weight or level of urgency for a project. The risks ranked lower during qualitative risk analysis cannot just be brushed aside and ignored. They made the list for a reason, and have the potential to impact the project. These low-level, non-critical risks are placed on a watchlist. The watchlist is a document the project manager will monitor intermittently throughout the project to ensure these risks don't creep into the project.

During the project, risk efforts may result in going back and changing components of the project management plan. For example, the risk process might involve the deletion of a piece of scope that was adding too much negative risk to the project. Therefore, the WBS and the project scope statement would have to be updated. Schedule and cost are also affected by the risk management process. Risk

Watchlist

Low-rated (non-critical) risks documented for intermittent monitoring and review throughout the life of the project management has the potential to result in many pieces of work becoming cheaper and faster. In addition, a team member who has estimated a certain piece of project work will be able to narrow the range of his estimate after the risks or uncertainties are diminished for that work.

Establishing Reserves

Risks will remain after the risk management effort. These risks must be budgeted and accounted for in the project management planning process. The risks that remain are added to the project cost and are included in the project schedule as reserves.

There can be two kinds of reserves on a project: a contingency reserve and a management reserve. The contingency reserve is a calculated amount of time and/or cost based on the specific risks that remain in the project after risk management. These are known risks with hard numbers associated with each one that measure the probability and impact of each risk. Contingency risk reserves can be supported and proven to management.

Management reserves are a percentage of the total project budget added on to the project to account for risks not identified. It is not an acceptable practice to have a management reserve without a contingency reserve.

Reserves are a required part of project management. The risk management process becomes advanced with the application of more complex techniques for identifying, assessing, and managing risk.

The following exercise illustrates how to calculate a contingency reserve for a project.

Exercise:

You are planning the installation of hardware and software to support unified communications throughout your company. After your risk management efforts to eliminate and reduce risks, you are left with the following risks that remain on the project. How much reserve would be needed for time on the project?

(For the sake of simplicity, we have only used four risk elements in this exercise.)

A. A 25 percent probability of a 4-day delay in receiving customer approval

B. A 10 percent probability that the equipment installation will take 40 days less than planned

C. A 50 percent probability that two telephone desk sets will need to be returned for poor quality, causing a 20-day delay

D. A 30 percent probability that a certain expert will become available to work on the project, resulting in a 9-day savings due to increased productivity

Answer:

Notice that some of these risks are opportunities (good things). A project manager needs to add time for threats (negative risks), and subtract time for opportunities.

A. This is a risk, so we add 25 percent × 4 days (+ 1 day)

B. This is an opportunity, so we subtract 10 percent × 40 days (- 4 days)

C. This is a risk, so we add 50 percent × 20 days (+ 10 days)

D. This is an opportunity, so we subtract 30 percent × 9 days (- 3 days)

The reserve should be: +(1) − (4) + (10) − (3) = 4 days.

The inclusion of this amount of time in the schedule is supported by describing the work it is meant to cover, just like normal project work. The additional time can also be supported by pointing out that the method of calculation allows for both risks and opportunities. It is not enough to just factor in the additional time (schedule risk) required. The project manager needs to be able to provide the costs (cost risk) associated with the additional time. What are the fully weighted salaries for the people putting in the additional time, or what would be the contract fees associated with using outside resources to mitigate the schedule risk?

Risk can affect every part of a project. Risk management is one of the last steps in the project planning process. It is not until after the WBS is created and after initial scheduling has been completed that many risks can be identified.

Throughout the Project

There are things that should be done related to risk while the project is underway. Consider:

- Including risks in communications and as a topic at team meetings
- Revisiting the watchlist of risks intermittently to make sure any of the risks previously classified as non-critical have not increased in ranking

- Looking for unexpected effects or consequences of risk events
- Reevaluating risk identification and qualitative and quantitative risk analysis when the project starts to deviate from the plan

 "We conduct 'what could go wrong' assessments at the end of every stage/ milestone of highly visible projects. … We put mitigation plans in place for high probability/high impact risks so that they wouldn't happen, or at least if they did happen we would minimize the impact."
– Alice Ferone, Associate Director for Global Business Services (GBS)
The Procter & Gamble Company
Read the complete interview with Alice Ferone in Appendix C.

Because risk management was done, the project manager will have substantially more time available while the work is in progress. Problems have already been identified and solutions planned. The following tricks will help you keep in control of the project.

 Use the risk register as a way to document data on risk so that it can be used as historical information on other projects.

 Management and other stakeholders often don't know how to properly be involved with a project and can therefore negatively impact the project by getting in the way. If this happens to you, you could assign these people some of the work to help look out for and manage risks.

 Keep the focus on risk by asking the following questions during team meetings. "What new risks have been identified this month?" "What parts of the project risk response plan need to be improved or changed?"

 Include how risks will be communicated in the communications management plan.

 Look for new risks when any changes are made to the project.

While the work is being done, the project manager's focus is on managing risks. When the project management processes are followed, the team knows what they need to do, buy-in has been received from the stakeholders, scope creep has been minimized, and the project management plan is as realistic as possible.

The benefits of risk management are:

- Improved control of the project
- Fewer hours spent dealing with problems
- More hours spent implementing risk response plans
- Overall decreased time and cost for the project
- Time to manage more projects
- Less stress

Team Members

Team members' involvement in risk management can include:

- Identify risks (threats AND opportunities)
- Work with stakeholders to identify their risks
- Determine probabilities and impacts
- Determine how to eliminate major risks
- Determine response plans, contingency plans, and fallback plans
- Own or manage some of the risks
- Implement risk response strategies when an identified risk occurs
- Let the project manager know when a problem occurs or may occur that was not identified as a risk
- Help to manage the reserve

Chapter Summary
Key Concepts

Risk management:

- Is a sequential and iterative process
- Includes increasing opportunities as well as decreasing threats
- Saves time and money on projects
- Improves project control

Questions for Discussion

How can risk management save time and money on a project?

Who should be involved in risk identification?

Name two types of risk reserve. What is the difference between the two?

How is a risk register used in project management?

Action Plan

1. What will you do differently in your real-world project management as a result of reading this chapter?
2. Add new items to your personal Tricks list in Chapter 2.

What Action?	Why?	By When?	Who Will Be Involved?	Who Will Be Affected?	Status

Saving the Failed or Failing IT Project

Goals of This Chapter

Upon completion of this chapter, you should be able to:

- Identify the characteristics of a failing project

- Know what steps to take to save a failing project

- Explain how to revive a failed project

Thomas J. Watson, the founder of IBM said, "If you want to be successful, double your failure rate." The point he was making is that growth comes from learning from your mistakes. As a human being, you can count on the fact that you will make mistakes. You will have projects that fail. You will be given projects that are failing. You have two choices: you can hang your head and walk away; or you can step back, take a deep breath, and figure out how to pull the project back on track.

Projects that fail share some or all of the following characteristics: poor requirements documentation, inadequate organizational support (in terms of executive sponsorship, money, or resources), poor team management, unrealistic scheduling, and ineffective communication. This book has addressed each of these issues across the chapters; however, look closely at the interviews in Appendix C. Each company, no matter how large or small, or what industry they serve, expects the project manager to prevent any project from completely failing. The larger the organization, the less tolerant it is of an IT project failure.

As one interviewee noted, there are times when a project manager just cannot do the job. In this situation, it is better to admit the lack of skill and ask for help from the executive sponsor. Under the same scenario, a different interviewee pointed to the value of using a project management coach. A third interviewee noted they would replace the project manager on the project and support additional training for the less skilled project manager. Communicating the need for assistance, as soon as it becomes evident the project manager is losing control, is the single, most frequently cited solution to a failing or failed project.

If you conduct an Internet search on the phrase "failed IT projects," you will find papers and research reports written by universities and large global consulting organizations citing staggering figures on the cost to business of failed infrastructure projects. Dig into the documents and the following items explaining the failures, no matter who conducted the research, bubble to the top:

- Lack of executive engagement
- Project did not fit into the company's overall business strategy
- Inadequate or incomplete project requirements information
- Poor communication between the project manager and the stakeholders
- Project manager was not certified, operating in a home-grown manner

This close examination of the top reasons IT projects fail illustrates the importance of the beginning processes of a project. Based on this list, three of the top five reasons for failed IT projects are due to improper planning and initial engagement. They fail before they even get started!

A project manager must take the time up front on a project to ensure wide executive support, develop a sound business case for doing the project, and ensure the product or service output requirements are solid.

An effective project manager possesses more than a project management certification and a portfolio of successful projects. A project manager has one of the few roles in a company that interacts with every level inside the organization, as well as with the clients. This person must have a highly refined EQ, or emotional quotient. EQ skills are the soft skills necessary to deal with people. A project manager who is new to a company should work closely with an internal mentor or coach. The mentor will be able to guide the new hire through the idiosyncrasies of the organization. Each company has its own culture with many nuances. Find someone who has been around a period of time and is willing to share this information. The more you know how to work within the company's culture, the more effective you will be in managing projects for the company.

Common Mistakes in Managing Projects

Over the course of the book, we have addressed common mistakes in managing projects. The following is a list of errors that contribute to project delays and failures. The list is not in order of importance.

The Blame Game

- Thinking an unrealistic schedule should be blamed on management, rather than on the project manager
- Not holding effective meetings, or bothering to ask those who attend meetings if the meetings were effective
- Blaming management for scope creep, requirement changes, and cost overruns

Misunderstanding the Tools

- Thinking project management is an optional activity
- Thinking software sold as "project management software" is intended to tell people how to manage projects
- Not using the best communication tools and methods for the stakeholders
- Not using the correct project management software for the scope of the project

Not Following the Project Management Process

- Not having a project charter
- Not obtaining broad executive buy-in
- Not using the project charter to remind people about what is the project
- Not having all the key requirements before starting work on the project
- Not keeping the project schedule updated, and not delivering that updated schedule to resource owners
- Not having a WBS for the project
- Failing to involve the entire team in creating the WBS
- Not identifying risks for the project
- Not realizing that time or cost estimates for the project cannot be completed without including the impacts of risk on the project
- Allowing team members to pad their project estimates
- Managing a program as if it was one project instead of many projects

- Not realizing there is a process to project management, and that steps taken early in the project prevent problems later in the project
- Thinking project management activities add time and cost, rather than saving time and cost
- Not having, or not using, records of lessons learned from past projects

Lack of Communication Activities

- Not developing a communications management plan
- Not including the stakeholders in project status communications
- Forgetting to include some stakeholders in the project planning and management processes
- Not identifying how each stakeholder wants to be communicated with
- Failing to recognize and reward successes throughout the project

What Steps Should a Project Manager Take When a Project Is in Jeopardy?

- Review the project's scope requirements compared to the WBS, WBS dictionary, and issue log.
- Meet with the executive sponsor to confirm the business value of the project to the company. The meeting should also include a complete review of the project charter, requirements, and scope documents.
- Meet with the project team and/or specific members who are not performing to learn what the hurdles are to completing work.
- Replace non-performing team members.
- Communicate, communicate, and communicate some more with all of the stakeholders to gather support, assistance, guidance, and additional funding if necessary, to reignite the enthusiasm that was behind the project initially.
- Be explicit with all of the stakeholders about the current state of the project and how it came to be in a state of decline.
- Develop a project recovery plan.
- Conduct a self assessment: Do you have the skills to manage this project? Are you using the right tools for the size and scope of the project? Are you committed and engaged with the project and its stakeholders?

How to Resurrect a Failed Project

Projects fail for a variety of reasons. Some IT projects, however, absolutely must be resurrected and completed. A company cannot let its communication systems be non-operational. Sales order entry must work accurately. Order entry and billing applications absolutely have to be integrated. Companies take on these types of IT projects to improve operations and business process flows. What should a project manager do when handed a business critical project that is being relaunched?

The short answer, start from scratch. Begin at the beginning and treat the project like a brand new project. Meet with the executive sponsor and stakeholders to validate the charter and business case for the project. Expect that the executive may be aggravated at the delays and expense of the project. Go into these meetings with a comprehensive understanding of what went wrong with the first efforts, and with a plan to ensure the relaunch of the project will avoid a similar fate. Expect that the requirements will have changed since the initial launch. Expect that the executives will want more communication and have the project on a tighter rein.

Set up a meeting with the project team members. Setting the tone of this meeting will be critical to achieving useful information. The goal is to understand what was working well in the execution process and what wasn't. Be sure everyone provides input into the discussion, exploring one item at a time. At the end of the meeting, offer each member the opportunity to contact you in confidence regarding their level of commitment to the project's relaunch. A project that is seeing a second coming does not have room for any member that is not wholly committed to its success.

As you take on and move through the project, the three things you need to focus on in almost an exaggerated mode are:

- Effective communication with all of the stakeholders
- Recognition of meeting milestones, exceptional performers, and thought leaders
- Delivering precisely against the project requirements

Chapter Summary
Key Concepts
Projects that fail share similar characteristics:

- The top reasons IT projects fail illustrate the importance of the beginning processes of a project
- If a project is failing or has failed, consider restarting the process from scratch to get back on track with a solid foundation

Questions for Discussion
Identify the top reasons IT projects fail.

What are some of the steps a project manager should take to get a failing project back on track?

What steps should be taken to relaunch a failed project?

Action Plan

1. What will you do differently in your real-world project management as a result of reading this chapter?
2. Add new items to your personal Tricks list in Chapter 2.

What Action?	Why?	By When?	Who Will Be Involved?	Who Will Be Affected?	Status

Goals of This Chapter

Upon completion of this chapter, you should be able to:

- Explain how to measure the business impact for a project

- Know when and how to use post-project monitoring

- Define the value of post-project reports and who should receive them

- Articulate how and why senior management should support project management methodologies and best practices

The project is finished. The end result has met the stakeholder requirements, and it came in on time and within budget. Now it is time to move on to the next project. But wait, not so fast. How do you know if the IT project has met the greatest goal of all: adding value to the business? Can the project manager unequivocally show that the business problem that spawned the project has been addressed and resolved?

Before a project manager sends off the final project report heralding in success, he or she better make sure the project really was successful in terms of adding value to the company. The value added is the bottom line; it is what really matters; it is why the project was chartered to begin with.

Are you familiar with the term "shelfware"? Shelfware is software that was purchased by a company, yet never used. It sits on a shelf gathering dust. It is a constant reminder of poor decision-making that probably led to a failed project. Software licensing is a huge expense for businesses. What happened frequently enough that a new word was added to the technology vernacular? In a nutshell: failure to adopt the new software.

Technology adoption failures occur on a regular basis. They happen across all of technology, not just with software. Lack of adoption happens for any of a number of reasons including poor or inadequate training of the users, the solution doesn't integrate with other business processes, the solution doesn't solve the business problem, or there is an existing solution with which everyone is already familiar.

How does a project manager avoid technology adoption failures and concurrently measure the project's impact on the business? Build the measurement metrics into the project management plan.

Measuring the effectiveness and business impact of the project should be rigorous, yet practical. It starts by knowing the baseline of the business problem being addressed with the project. For example, if customer satisfaction is down, then the baseline unit of measure is customer satisfaction as currently measured by the company. A project is chartered to provide unified communications for sales and service personnel. When the project is completed, customer satisfaction surveys are sent at defined intervals, maybe quarterly in this case, to measure the percentage of uptick in sales and service responsiveness. This is measuring the business impact of the unified communications project.

Business impact can be measured in three ways—qualitative, quantitative, and blended. Qualitative research is the process of collecting in-depth data from a limited number of sources. In our customer satisfaction scenario, the firm would engage with a defined percentage of customers up and down the satisfaction baseline. The company might send satisfaction surveys on a quarterly basis, or conduct telephone interviews. It may consider going to customer sites or bringing customers to the home office. Qualitative measures are conducted with the same participants, at regular intervals, for a fixed period of time. If the charter of the unified communications solution was to improve customer satisfaction X-percent over two years, then the qualitative research would be conducted over that period of time.

Quantitative research uses statistical analysis on large bodies of data. The data can come from surveys and data extraction applied to company databases. Using the unified communications/customer satisfaction scenario, the company would extract historical customer satisfaction data from its data stores. It would also survey most all of its customers upon project completion and at a defined interval, for example, six months. Using statistical analysis, the data trend from the historical information would be compared with the newest data, post-project. Quantitative research results are shown in a graphical format illustrating a before/during/after project implementation.

The blended model uses both quantitative and qualitative research methods to measure business impact. This is the most accurate method of measuring business impact, but it is also the most time consuming and expensive.

Other metrics used for measuring business value impact include return on investment, internal and/or external adoption rate, and revenue metrics such as production cost reductions directly related to the bottom line. Measuring the business impact of a project helps a firm better understand the value of its technology investments.

The Importance of Building a Post-Project Monitoring System

The post-project monitoring system should be viewed as a temporary arrangement. Monitoring could last as little as a week. During the monitoring process, the project manager is watching for adoption rate of the technology, any bugs or problems with the new application, and any other issues.

The interviews in Appendix C illustrate the larger the company, the less likely that the project implementation team will also conduct the post-project monitoring. The largest companies wrap up a project, then turn it over to another group or division to monitor and support. The monitoring system used by a service group is a relatively permanent set of metrics aimed at measuring the business value or impact of the project on the company. Occasionally the project team will get called back to make minor adjustments, especially with software, but generally speaking, "done is done."

For the smaller companies that were interviewed, post-project monitoring was encased in a wrapper of customer relationship management and/or business strategy. These companies are working on growing their businesses, so it is logical that for them, post-project monitoring is a fundamental component to project management, customer touch, and customer retention.

There are other situations where a firm may not conduct post-project monitoring. For example, companies that have a managed services organization will try to sell customers post-project monitoring as a service. It would be counterproductive for the firm if the professional services group who did the implementation provided ongoing monitoring instead of handing the account off to the managed services team.

Reports and Who Gets Them

Reporting and who gets those reports were discussed in Chapter 12. The ongoing project reports and status updates are sent to the executive sponsor and project stakeholders. But who should receive the final reports? The report that addresses the business problems the project solved, with the metrics to demonstrate the business impact? The report that summarizes the outstanding efforts of the team in meeting milestones, goals, and objectives on a consistent basis? Who should receive the final report that includes salient quotes from the customer, whether an internal or external customer, on the professionalism, skills, and cooperative nature of the project team? The report singing the project's praises is sent to the executive team, the project team members' direct management, and the company's marketing communications department. This is the type of information marketing communications delights in receiving. It can be used to help build company morale, reach new external customers, and enhance the firm's community standing.

The other report that covers the discussion items, line by line, from the lessons learned meeting, should go to the executive sponsor and executive team, to the executive who asked for the project and supported its charter. The lessons learned report should also go to each team member and their direct manager. Finally, a copy of this lessons learned report must be included with the project file and stored in the historic projects archives.

The information gleaned from lessons learned meetings, both positive and negative information, helps everyone on the team to grow. Even the seasoned players can learn a few new tricks from the new hires regarding best practices or emerging technologies. We have discussed the value of having this information available for other project managers, too. Any resources or assets that improve project implementations are invaluable. Consider how valuable the project documents could be for projects that have been incrementalized, broken down into smaller components to be rolled out across individual workgroups. Think of all the mistakes that can be avoided with each succeeding implementation. The lessons learned meeting and subsequent report is not an activity that can or should be deemed optional. These activities are part of a project manager's repertoire of best practices.

How the Boss Can Help

After studying this material, it may seem like the project manager is shouldering a heavy burden. The project manager acts as a maestro, coordinating and facilitating all the different resources needed to take a project from concept to completion. There are numerous ways executive management can support the team to be successful in its endeavors. These include:

1. Support the creation and retention of project records. Historical records include, at a minimum, the WBS, estimates, risks, and lessons learned for every project. These records are used to train new-to-the-company project managers, and assist in better planning, estimating, and management of future projects.

2. Provide a project charter with clear goals and objectives. Include a description of the project, the project manager's name, clearly defined quantitative goals and objectives (i.e., a 10 percent improvement), and an explanation of why the project is being done. The project charter serves as a "target" for the project. The goals and objectives provide a way to measure success.

3. Protect projects from outside influences, changes, and resource poaching.

4. Allow teams the time to properly plan projects. Teams need time to plan projects in order to achieve substantial decreases in project length and cost. A project schedule cannot be delivered in only a few days.

5. Ensure a finalized scope of work before the project starts. There is little excuse for not having a finalized scope of work. Changes made later can cost 100 times more.

6. Prioritize projects within the company or department. Everyone should know which projects are number one, two, three, etc., in priority at any time within your organization.

7. Require that project management tools, methodologies and best practices be used. Your support of project management is critical for it to be adopted in the company. Focus on the project charter, the WBS, and risk management.

8. Run the project management team slightly below 100 percent capacity. Overtime is not an option, because any one problem will cause massive problems on all projects. Having breathing room also prevents team member burnout.

9. Know that you cannot get something for nothing. Any changes in scope, time, and/or cost will impact project scope, time, and/or cost. Do not allow people to ask for little extras and not expect to pay for them.

10. Back the project team when it comes under criticism. It may appear like the team is dragging its feet as it takes the necessary time to gather all of the requirements and to build the elements that make up the overall project plan. Defending the pre-project work will help to ensure the team consistently follows project management methodologies and best practices.

11. Support project management certifications, tools, and methodologies as the business enablers that they are. Encourage and support employees interested in project management to obtain appropriate certification and ongoing training to keep their skills current and sharp.

Team Members

Team members also have a role in driving the business value of project management methodologies and best practices. In one of our training sessions, a group of team members stopped the class and said, "None of our managers know any of this." They were asked by the training leader what they were going to do about it. After taking some time to think, they decided to take a copy of the free tip on the RMC Web site (www.rmcproject.com/IT) from which this chapter is derived, have all the team members sign it, and give it to their manager. The manager had time to read and think about how project management could help the company, and how she could facilitate its use. The situation wasn't confrontational, and demonstrated the commitment of the team to finding ways to improve how they worked on projects. Information breeds understanding. With information, this manager was able to improve her management activities.

What can your team do about improving things in your company?

Chapter Summary
Key Concepts

- Measuring the effectiveness and business impact of the project should be rigorous, yet practical
- End-of-project reports have value across multiple departments in the company
- Executive management support of project management processes is essential to organizations

Questions for Discussion

Explain the value of measuring a project's business impact.

| |
| |
| |
| |
| |

Should all IT projects have a post-project monitoring system set up? Why or why not?

| |
| |
| |
| |
| |

How can executive management support the project manager and the team?

Action Plan

1. What will you do differently in your real-world project management as a result of reading this chapter?
2. Add new items to your personal Tricks list in Chapter 2.

What Action?	Why?	By When?	Who Will Be Involved?	Who Will Be Affected?	Status

Next Steps

This book was designed as an introduction to the most important aspects of project management, the methodology, and numerous best practice ideas. By reading the book, completing the exercises, and answering the questions at the end of each chapter, you have gained a solid foundation of knowledge to immediately apply to your next project.

To further improve your IT project management effectiveness, work on the skills you have learned from this book for a year or so. After mastering the basics of project management, come back to this chapter to learn the next steps to becoming a project management expert.

Assessing Your Project Management Skills

 Ask your team members.

> If you really want to know how well you are doing in applying project management methodologies and best practices, ask your team members and your coach.
>
> Many people will not feel comfortable addressing this topic in a group setting or even in a one-on-one setting, especially if they have criticisms. In order to get an honest answer, express your sincere interest in hearing their opinions and then offer many ways they can provide feedback (e.g., by e-mail, a phone call, or in writing). Make sure there is an option for them to reply to you anonymously.
>
> Ask your team members for specific comments regarding the project management concepts presented in this book. You will be surprised to see just how fast they respond to your request, because chances are they have been thinking about this since you started to use professional project management techniques.

The topics to include in your survey are, "How have I done in…"

- Understanding the project management process
- Breaking the work into projects
- Obtaining, creating, and using historical information
- Identifying and managing stakeholders
- Creating and keeping focus on the project charter
- Creating and managing the project scope statement
- Creating and updating the WBS
- Identifying and managing risk on the project
- Creating and updating the communications management plan
- Avoiding the common errors that can ruin our careers
- Getting our bosses to work on the things they should be doing

Implement the improvements suggested by your team members before moving on to increasing your knowledge.

Next Steps to Expanding Project Management Skills

If you are ready to take the next steps in your project management skills growth, consider this list of suggestions.

Take a Class

RMC Project Management focuses on teaching you what you need to know to improve your real-world project management skills. Review the RMC Web site, www.rmcproject.com, for online and instructor-led training on more advanced project management topics. Courses to consider as next steps include:

- **Tricks of the Trade® for Project Management** Fill the gaps in your knowledge of basic and advanced skills in project management.
- **Tricks of the Trade® for Risk Management** Risk management can make the biggest improvement in your overall project management activities after you learn the basics.
- **15 Attributes of the Most Successful Project Managers** Learn advanced skills of the best project managers from around the world.

Continue to Develop Your Project Management Skills

- Improve your meeting management skills
- Create quality standards to help manage and control the project
- Measure progress, including earned value techniques
- Expand your knowledge of change control techniques
- Learn more about conflict resolution techniques
- Read about advanced topics, including expanded discussions on estimating time and cost
- Identify and manage float
- Use Monte Carlo analysis to determine the probability of completing the project on any specific day for any specific amount of moneyFollow the Project Management Process

Follow the Project Management Process

Continue to assimilate and apply the step-by-step process of project management as described in Rita's Process Chart shown earlier and repeated on the following page.

INITIATING	PLANNING (This is the only process group with a set order)	EXECUTING	MONITORING & CONTROLLING	CLOSING
▶ Select project manager	▶ Determine how you will do planning—part of all management plans	▶ Execute the work according to the PM plan	▶ Take action to control the project	▶ Confirm work is done to requirements
▶ Determine company culture and existing systems	▶ Finalize requirements	▶ Produce product scope	▶ Measure performance against the performance measurement baseline	▶ Complete procurement closure
▶ Collect processes, procedures, and historical information	▶ Create project scope statement	▶ Request changes	▶ Measure performance against other metrics determined by the project manager	▶ Gain formal acceptance of the product
▶ Divide large projects into phases	▶ Determine what to purchase	▶ Implement only approved changes		▶ Complete final performance reporting
▶ Understand the business case	▶ Determine team	▶ Ensure common understanding	▶ Determine variances and if they warrant a change request	▶ Index and archive records
▶ Uncover initial requirements and risks	▶ Create WBS and WBS dictionary	▶ Use the work authorization system	▶ Influence the factors that cause changes	▶ Update lessons learned knowledge base
▶ Create measurable objectives	▶ Create activity list	▶ Continuously improve		▶ Hand off completed product
▶ Develop project charter	▶ Create network diagram	▶ Follow processes	▶ Request changes	▶ Release resources
▶ Identify stakeholders	▶ Estimate resource requirements	▶ Perform quality assurance	▶ Perform integrated change control	
▶ Develop stakeholder management strategy	▶ Estimate time and cost	▶ Perform quality audits	▶ Approve or reject changes	
	▶ Determine critical path	▶ Acquire final team	▶ Inform stakeholders of approved changes	
	▶ Develop schedule	▶ Manage people	▶ Manage configuration	
	▶ Develop budget	▶ Evaluate team and project performance	▶ Create forecasts	
	▶ Determine quality standards, processes, and metrics	▶ Hold team-building activities	▶ Gain acceptance of interim deliverables from the customer	
	▶ Create process improvement plan	▶ Give recognition and rewards	▶ Perform quality control	
	▶ Determine all roles and responsibilities	▶ Use issue logs	▶ Report on project performance	
	▶ Plan communications	▶ Facilitate conflict resolution	▶ Perform risk audits	
	▶ Perform risk identification, qualitative and quantitative risk analysis, and risk response planning	▶ Send and receive information	▶ Manage reserves	
	▶ Go back—iterations	▶ Hold meetings	▶ Administer procurements	
	▶ Prepare procurement documents	▶ Select sellers		
	▶ Finalize the "how to execute and control" parts of all management plans			
	▶ Develop final PM plan and performance measurement baseline that are realistic			
	▶ Gain formal approval of the plan			
	▶ Hold kickoff meeting			

Appendix

Business Process Improvement Standards
Six Sigma and ITIL

In an effort to retain control of the entire IT environment and ensure on-going interoperability, several IT-specific, standards-based process improvement methodologies have been developed. Organizations that use IT-centric process improvement methodologies understand the value defined methodologies bring to the situation. IT-specific process improvement methodologies are complementary to project management methodologies. Organizations that use both methodologies (IT and project management) have grasped the value good process definitions bring to the company including faster, better execution, enhanced results, and improved company performance.

Six Sigma Process Improvements

Six Sigma Process Improvements was developed in the 1980s. Motorola is generally credited with its development. The process describes how the management of product and service delivery should be implemented based on statistical analysis of data inputs against defined company objectives. The end goal is to achieve a statistical state of six sigma, or 99.9997% efficiency. This works out to a maximum defect rate of 3.4 units per million outputs.

The Six Sigma project management methodology emphasizes continuous process improvement as illustrated in the figure below. While it was originally developed for the manufacturing industry, today organizations use the methodology across many parts of the company such as finance and human resources. The model takes a strict project management approach that includes:

Define Establish the process and its inputs and outputs, set up the team and plan the project

Measure Gather baseline data to establish the current state and identify potential causes of variation, waste, and defects

Analyze Closely examine the relationships between the inputs and the outputs to identify potential causes of deviations from acceptable outputs

Improve Identify potential solutions to correct the deviation, design the new process incorporating the improvements

- **Control** Establish the controls and monitors that will sustain the improvements over time
- **Transfer** Apply the learning gained on this project to other areas in the business, potentially multiplying the benefits across the company

Benefits and Drawbacks of Implementing Six Sigma Process Improvements

The benefits of implementing Six Sigma are measurable and can be substantial. Six Sigma emphasizes process improvement. As a result, the benefits include reduced cycle-times, less waste of raw materials, and more reliable and consistent outputs of products.

There are numerous drawbacks an organization must consider when evaluating the six sigma process improvement methodology. First, it was designed for the manufacturing environment. As a result, it is optimized for that environment and is not typically considered an ideal solution for other strategic parts of the company where creativity is more highly valued over templates and strict execution models such as marketing or research and development.

Additional drawbacks include costly and time intensive training and implementation. Furthermore, the rigidity of the method and its tight statistical analysis inhibits an organization's nimbleness. By being completely data-driven, Six Sigma squeezes out any room for experience or subjectivity. As a result, the entire process is only as good as the quality and accuracy of the initial inputs.

ITIL

ITIL (IT Infrastructure Library) is the newest IT process improvement methodology. It was developed in the early 1990s by the British government. Since its initial release there have been two major revisions to the methodology with the most current version called ITILv3.

ITIL was developed specifically for the IT environment. ITIL consists of seven core areas: service support, service delivery, security management, planning to implement service management, business perspective, applications management, and ICT (information, communications and technology) infrastructure management.

The ITIL framework provides a structured, scalable, best practices process roadmap that readily scales up or down to meet the needs of any size company. The framework also adjusts to service delivery models such as in-house or via the cloud. As a result of the flexibility of the framework and its exclusive focus on the IT environment, ITIL has become the global de facto process standard.

Benefits and Drawbacks to Implementing ITILv3 Process Improvement Methods

Like Six Sigma, the benefits to an organization implementing ITILv3 can be substantial. ITILv3 provides a single, definable, repeatable, and highly scalable documented framework for IT best practices that spans the entire IT team. The emphasis of ITILv3 is on reducing IT costs, and factually justifies the costs associated with IT implementations. More importantly, ITILv3 supports the IT group's need to be able to take advantage of changing business environments, emerging technologies, and evolving regulatory compliance.

ITIL may sound like the perfect solution to managing IT implementations, but it does come with a few drawbacks. First, IT must have end-to-end visibility across the company's infrastructure. This is typically not possible when rogue workgroups elect to implement a technology for their own benefit, thereby creating islands of technology isolation that impact the holistic view. Should the workgroup elect to put their applications and data in the cloud, which is frequently happening in groups that need intensive collaboration support, the IT team is completely blind and unable to provide service assurance, backups, and data recovery.

Mobility and intermittent network access also add challenge to ITILv3 implementations. Smart phones, laptops, and VPN access make it virtually impossible for IT to be able to keep track of devices and the applications running on them in real-time. Intermittent access impedes IT's ability to effectively measure service levels and service efficiencies across the core areas of ITIL, weakening the value proposition of using ITIL.

Appendix

Project Management Software Considerations

There are dozens of project management software applications available in the market. They all perform basically the same function of time and resource management, but depending on the complexity of your environment, one solution may be better for you than another.

The choice of project management software is based on how you approach projects. Are all of the resources in-house and able to access the same secure network? Do you use contractors to provide expertise on some project components? Are workers localized or geographically scattered? Is the project part of a larger project? Is the project expected to be span several weeks or several years? Answers to these questions will help to determine what project management application you select.

Features to consider when evaluating project management tools include:

- Task management
- Recurring tasks
- File sharing
- File storage
- Reporting functions
- Progress charting
- Client access
- Subcontractor task assignment capabilities
- Time tracking
- Security
- Invoicing
- Budgeting
- Notebook or whiteboard space
- Multiple project support
- Project-based to-do list
- Personnel commenting space
- Milestones
- E-mail integration

Most of the features in this list are fundamental, but there are a couple of items that need a bit more explanation. *Progress charting* provides the project manager a rapid glance status check of the overall project as well as where each of the active contributors are relative to the deliverable deadlines. This feature allows the project manager to be proactive in adding resources if necessary before a failed deliverable becomes a problem, potentially impacting the overall project's success.

Personnel commenting space is more important than it may seem at first pass. Commenting space allows project personnel the opportunity to provide status notes and additional information beyond completed/not completed milestone check off. If someone is waiting for a part, and that part will not ship for three weeks, the project manager needs to be aware of the situation. Personnel commenting space enhances communication between the project manager and those performing the work.

E-mail integration is especially important for project teams that do not get together on a regular basis or are geographically dispersed. E-mail integration allows the project manager to set up automated status queries as milestones approach. By automating some basic project monitoring functionality, a single project manager is able to support more concurrent projects. Communication is also improved by removing the latency associated with having to manually e-mail team members for status updates.

Project Management Tool Implementation Methods: Strengths and Weaknesses of Each Model

When selecting a project management application, it is important to understand how it will be implemented. Will your company buy the software and install it in-house? Will you use a hosted service? Will the organization use the Software as a Service (SaaS) model? The implementation method will influence the price points of the tool. Pricing ranges from free to several thousand dollars to pay-per-use models.

In-house tools are those purchased and installed at the company. The monitoring, management, and integration of the application with other applications is the responsibility of the company's IT department. The IT department is also responsible for providing secure access to contractors and subcontractors.

Hosted tools are owned by the company, but installed at a third party facility. The hosting company handles all of the maintenance and support of the application, and typically can also provide some nominal level of integration with other applications you may be using. The hosting company also provides secure access and identity management.

Cloud computing or Software as a Service (SaaS) has the application owned and installed at the service provider's facility. SaaS providers are software savvy and can support an organization's need for integration with other applications or to blend applications in a mash-up such as a physical map, time zones, and key functions of the project management tool. Companies pay on a per-user basis. Application access and security is the responsibility of the SaaS vendor.

1. In-House Implementation

Strengths	Weaknesses
Software can be integrated with other in-house applications	Must purchase software licenses
Project history knowledge base stored in-house	Software upgrades and patches expensive
Application usage knowledge may be in-house	Access limitations for contractors and subcontractors

2. Hosted Implementation

Strengths	Weaknesses
Software can be integrated with other hosted applications	Must purchase software licenses
User elasticity, buy only the licenses needed at any point in time	Software upgrades and patches expensive
Secure access available to contractors and subcontractors	Project history knowledge base stored at service provider facility

3. In the Cloud or SaaS

Strengths	Weaknesses
Software can be integrated and even "mashed up" with other SaaS applications	Viability of SaaS provider must be monitored
User elasticity, buy only number of user access points needed	SaaS provider must have SAS 70 Type II certification to ensure security
No software purchases, software is always current, patched, and maintained	

Appendix

![REAL WORLD IT] **Real-World IT Interviews**

Introduction

To gain a glimpse into organizations using the tools and methodologies discussed in this book, we interviewed companies applying project management in their real-world IT projects. Our goal was to understand the driving factors behind the decision to embrace project management best practices, and to gain insight into their experiences.

Representatives from the following organizations participated in the interviews:

- CH2M HILL (www.ch2mhill.com) a privately held engineering firm headquartered in Englewood, Colorado, USA [see page 207]
- Clikthrough, Inc. (www.clikthrough.com) a 20-person start-up firm operating in the emerging interactive video market headquartered in San Francisco, California, USA [see page 215]
- Evolution Technology Group (www.ETG.net) a medical industry outsourcing IT company based in Birmingham, Alabama, USA [see page 223]
- The Procter & Gamble Company (www.pg.com) a publicly-traded consumer goods enterprise based in Cincinnati, Ohio, USA [see page 229]
- SunGard Higher Education (www.sungardhe.com) a privately held, Fortune 500 company based in providing IT infrastructure and services, software, and processing solutions Wayne, Pennsylvania, USA [see page 237]

You will note that representatives of small and large, public and private organizations were interviewed. It is rare to be able to gain visibility into a firm's internal operations, and we are deeply indebted to those who participated in these interviews. Read the interviews and realize that their success is rooted in a tightly managed, focused implementation that emphasizes the support of strategic business objectives. Technology was implemented across each of the organizations for the benefits of reducing costs, improving efficiencies, and supporting the core business.

Here are some of significant findings that span all the interviews:

- Planning is fundamental to project success.
- There is value in the disciplined approach to using the project management methodology.
- Frequent, effective communication of project status is critical to the project's success.
- Well-honed soft skills are a valuable asset for project managers.
- Using project management methodologies for IT initiatives demonstrably improves the value of IT for the company or client.

These interviews support the fact that businesses can leverage project management methodologies for IT to achieve significant measurable gains across implementation times, improved process flows, and improved cash flows. A company can increase its business process efficiencies, intellectual property, and competitive advantage in any business climate.

Throughout the book, we have noted that project management is as much an art as it is a science. From the artist's perspective, there are many shades of gray. The artistic side of project management comes through clearly in these interviews. Where the science of project management, as defined by various project management standards, says one thing, the interview subjects approach some tools and reporting in a noticeably different manner. Notable differences also appear based on company size, age, and vertical markets.

As you read through the interviews you will see how the start-up firms are just beginning to use project management tools and methodologies, and have not yet adopted the entire process. The large, established firms use a rigorous process, but still apply modifications that better meet their business needs. This is not to say that any of the firms are performing project management "wrong." These deltas clearly and unequivocally demonstrate that project management for IT, whether applied as a beginner or as a seasoned professional, adds significant value to the IT project and to the company overall. Obviously, the more rigorous the application of project management tools and methodologies, the greater the value delivered to the project and the company.

In the words of Lewis Carroll in Alice in Wonderland, ""Begin at the beginning," the King said, very gravely, "and go on till you come to the end: then stop." All of the interviewees, whether new to project management or seasoned veterans, noted they continue to learn and grow professionally in their project management skills, but they began at the beginning just as you are doing with this book.

 **CH2M HILL**
www.ch2mhill.com

The following is based on a personal interview with Ronald Nickell, Senior Project Manager, PMO.

Company Background

- CH2M HILL is a privately-held engineering firm.
- The company was founded in January, 1946 in Corvallis, Oregon, USA by Fred Merryfield, an Oregon State College civil engineering professor, and three of his student protégées; Holly Cornell, James Howland, and T. Burke Hayes. The company's founding was opportunistic, leveraging the demand for talented engineers in the post-WWII economy.
- The company is headquartered in Englewood, Colorado, USA.
- It has approximately 25,000 employees spread across facilities on nearly every continent.
- Within the larger company is a 1,300 employee organization of IT and project management professionals. These people are dedicated to providing the support necessary to ensure the project constraints, including scope, cost, and time, are maintained for every project in which the company engages.

From its inception, technology-based engineering and consulting solutions have been core to CH2M HILL. The company has grown from a wastewater treatment firm to a multinational engineering company with expertise in every area of engineering including Superfund cleanup, Panama Canal expansion, and the world's first fully sustainable city, Masdar City in the UAE.

Why Project Management Is Necessary for this Company

Every project undertaken by the CH2M HILL engineers is built on the foundation of project management tools and methodologies.

At CH2M HILL, nearly every contract is a program; a collection of incremental projects that make up a substantially larger output. Programs run from a few weeks up to a decade or more. There can be a large number of people, both inside and outside the firm, engaged with each program. Project management ensures every party associated with a project is up-to-date on the status of the work, who is accountable for work package fulfillment, and how all of the different teams' efforts influence and impact every milestone along the path to completion. In addition, project management enables the program manager to see, at a glance, how the incremental projects are enabling the larger program outputs.

Executive Management Attitudes on Project Management Certifications

CH2M HILL is a company built on managing projects. According to Nickell, "Our company engages in projects that specifically require a PMP-certified project manager as one of the terms of each contract. CH2M HILL management seeks project management certification as part of our recruitment process."

Within the IT team, the firm will hire based on technical skills over project management skills, but strongly encourages and supports new hires to obtain PMP certification. The company also has a budget for employees to attend courses and conferences, and subscribes to online PMP training programs, ensuring their skills are kept sharp and current.

Project and Portfolio Management

CH2M HILL's total project portfolio is managed at the corporate level. The IT group's projects generally roll up into larger programs; therefore, they are influenced and directed by the corporate-level program managers. Nickell stated:

- "As a general guideline, the company uses an ROI methodology to prioritize projects within the overall portfolio. We in IT follow their lead and are rerouted based on the program-level directives."
- "The company also weighs opportunities to get into new businesses that align with the company's strategic objectives. Historically, this is how the company enters into any new business opportunity. On a current level, opportunities that present themselves in the alternative energy market, assuming they meet the ROI target, would be candidates for being prioritized."

The project portfolio within the IT group, on average, consists of 200 to 300 projects annually. Each of the projects is managed by a project manager, and approximately 90 percent of them are managed using project management software. The remaining 10 percent do not require the use of software because they are infrastructure projects where the team members or managers can manage them on an ad hoc basis. These are initiatives where the team member has extensive experience and the activities are repetitive to IT, such as building out server farms. Nickell noted:

- "We have numerous mega-programs that have dozens of IT projects associated with them. At the next level, we have approximately ten times as many large projects. There are a substantial number of smaller IT projects that run much shorter durations, maybe a month or two."

- "Each IT project manager is responsible for between two and four projects concurrently depending on what else is going on. For example, if a PM is working on a super-project, he or she is focusing on a single project. In other situations, PMs may have four to six projects on their plate because the projects are small and can be easily managed by a single person."

- "The average project life cycle is around six months of time. Of course, there are much shorter ones. We tend to operate on 90 day cycles. On average it takes two cycles to get a project done. Sometimes it is only one cycle, but on the other hand, with the huge programs it may take 12 cycles to get the project done. So, I would say that the average IT project life cycle is around six months."

Benefits of Using Project Management Tools and Methodologies

At CH2M HILL, project management tools and methodologies are critical to its ongoing success. The myriad of project tools used enables the firm to effectively and efficiently manage its smallest projects as well as some of the largest projects in the world. The more efficient CH2M HILL is in taking a project from concept to completion, the greater the overall benefits are to the firm, including return on investment and opportunity costs. Nickell commented:

- "IT is generally one part of a much larger project. If we don't get our piece done on time and in budget, the construction engineers are waiting for us and we are probably having huge impacts on their delivery schedule."

- "IT project management helps reduce or remove the risk of cost overruns and the political consequences that go with that."

At CH2M HILL, projects range in size and scope from less than 30 days to up to a decade or more. There isn't one software tool capable of supporting this breadth of scope. The net result is that each project manager has to be fluent with several different tools such as Daptive, Microsoft Project, Maximo, and Primavera. It is important that each PM use the correct tool for the project being managed. A lot of time could be wasted if the tool is too large or too small for the project at hand. Fortunately, the general concepts of project management are consistent across all of the tools.

Nickell emphatically stated, "You need to make sure that the tools and methodologies you are using are the right fit for the project you are delivering."

Defining Project Success

For CH2M HILL, Nickell said:

- "The company uses standard project management metrics including CPI (cost performance index) and SPI (schedule performance index) for each project."
- "We focus on earned value metrics during the course of a project. Business measures and (key performance) indicators (KPIs) are how we measure project success. They compare costs of the actual versus the budgeted; they compare the scheduled time versus the time it took to complete."

Establishing Work Breakdown Structures, Managing Expectations, and Improving Communication Flows

CH2M HILL uses several different project management tools, including Microsoft's SharePoint for collaboration and information sharing. This model provides everyone immediate access to project information including the WBS, problem logs, reports, and project status. In addition, the SharePoint site acts as storage for establishing historical project archives and making the project data readily available to all members of the team no matter where they reside geographically.

Nickell pointed out that when the WBS is developed using any of the company's project management software tools, there is a graphical interface that shows what is going on with the project. He notes:

- "With these tools, you can create pictures to embed into other documents which you can then send to the clients or managers on the larger projects to report on the status of the IT part of the project."
- "With Primavera, our project management tool for very large projects, the program managers have automatic visibility into what is going on with the IT component. They manage our project as a subproject of the mega-program."
- "All these tools are good for communicating. Everyone is looking at the same plan. They all understand as things change, as projects do, where their timeframe might need to change."
- "If there is a charter change, then you are going to have to revamp the plan, and come back to the stakeholders and talk to them about what the new plan is and any changes in cost, time, and scope. You're going to have to do some real quick project replanning."

- The goal of project management is to deliver the best solution for the client's business. This may require some changes in the original scope. The sooner these change requirements are recognized, the faster they can be addressed, and the lower the impact on the project."

How Project Management Helps Mitigate Pitfalls

At CH2M HILL, Nickell notes that managing project risk comes down to effective communication with the appropriate constituents. Specifically, Nickell suggests the following in these common scenarios:

- If a key sponsor or stakeholder departs:
  - ▸ The first thing to do is to go meet with the new people who are coming in; the new person or people who are now going to be the stakeholders. You need to talk with them about what the project has been doing, what you're doing now, and what you're intending to do to deliver the project. You have to be very detailed in this conversation about what you are trying to accomplish, what you think the goals of the project are, and what is the project's charter."
- If there is a major change to the project:
  - ▸ You are going to have to revamp the plan, and come back to the stakeholders and talk to them about the new plan and any changes or impacts to cost, time, scope, etc."
  - ▸ "You have got to get your team members on track immediately with what the new plan is."
  - ▸ "Mitigating problems effectively revolves around processes and procedures, and best practices of regularly dialoguing with the client. Open the lines of communication with your client to make sure you understand what changes are taking place in their business processes that could impact the project's original deliverable. You are looking for the nuances of changes that would directly impact the project's deliverables. The goal of project management is to deliver the best solution for the client's business. This may require some changes in the original scope. The sooner these change requirements are recognized, the faster they can be addressed, and the lower the impact on the project."

Post-Project

The need for ongoing post-project reports depends on how integrated the IT projects are with each other. For example, if the project is part of a larger program, there is going to be a greater need for ongoing status reports than if the project is independent of follow-on projects.

At CH2M HILL, the lessons learned sessions are a critical part of bringing a project to closure. Nickell advises: "The project manager needs to set a positive tone to the session. If you come in with a tone of negativity, the lessons learned will turn into a complaining session. Start by reminding the attendees that everyone needs to treat everyone else with respect. Let them know that they are there to try to understand things so that it can be better the next time. If you set the tone like that, then the whole meeting will follow in a civil and positive manner."

Nickell noted the following value for the company that comes from the sessions:

- "It is very important to sit down at the end of the project, and take the appropriate extra time with everybody on the team and have a discussion about how the project went from everybody's point of view, whether that's the tester who was at the tail end of the project or the requirements analyst who was at the front end of the project, or the salesperson who sold it. It is not a matter of gaining one point of view; it is a desire to gain a comprehensive view. On every project, everyone must provide feedback because when we do, collectively we continuously improve upon the process."
- "Our lessons learned sessions are where every part of the organization that has to do with IT comes to understand what their individual actions do to impact the overall project. It is a holistic system view."
- "Getting everybody into a room or on a conference call and having a discussion, from their perspective, of where things went well or didn't go well helps you in the very next project to do better."
- "You have got to take that data and get it out to other people who are doing similar projects to the project you are doing. If you don't, then other teams are going to be doomed to make those same mistakes."

Words of Wisdom

As a seasoned, senior IT project manager at CH2M HILL, Ronald Nickell has a platinum-grade perspective on project management. He and his team offer the following advice to those beginning their project management careers:

- "The first thing is to get good requirements and make sure that you test appropriately at the unit, system, and system test and user levels. If you don't get good requirements, you are not going to ever be able to deliver what the people want. It is really hard to get good requirements because users tend to want to quickly tell you. They understand what their problems are and they think it is perfectly obvious to you, too. But it usually is not. So, sitting down and getting good requirements and getting requirements sign-off is the key. Spend a little money up front before you have people developing so that you're not having to refactor things later in the project when your budgets and time are truly fixed."

- "Keep your sponsor up to date. If you are going to give the sponsor bad news, it is better to give bad news early than it is to give bad news late when there is no opportunity for changes or course corrections you need to make. Be honest with him or her. When things are going bad, be honest with them and tell them things are not going well. If you do that, you will be more successful than you would be if you try to hold things close to the vest and try to solve the problems. There are always political issues around that, but you are always better off to communicate early."

- "The right people and the right processes on a project are more important than having any project management software application. If you can get the right people who can do the jobs, they are self starters that can do what they need to do, you don't need that many tools to manage the project. If your processes and your best practices are good, you are in good shape. If you don't have them or they are kind of flaky, you will probably have problems."

- "On the communication side, make sure you are communicating with your team every day as to what's going on, where things are going, and how you see things progressing. If you are supporting your team, your team will support you. You are nothing without your team. You are not out there doing this development yourself. Make sure you are protecting them. Communication is the key to keeping your project going. Communicate with your team, communicate with your sponsors, communicate with your upper management and make sure everybody is on the same page of where the project is."

Clikthrough, Inc.
www.clikthrough.com

The following is based on a personal interview with Abe McCallum, CEO.

Company Background

Video is rapidly becoming one of the largest communication mediums for businesses of all sizes. Web sites have been developed, devoted exclusively to sharing video and video clips; companies use video to engage with customers and prospects; and most social networking sites support video links. The issue, however, is that the players up and down the video value chain have been unable to measure and monetize their efforts.

- Clikthrough, Inc. is a 20-person start-up firm operating in the emerging interactive video market.
- The company launched in 2007 with its first round of funding.
- The firm is headquartered in San Francisco, California, USA. Its core team is in the United States. It also leverages offshore development teams and a bevy of contractors for product development.
- Clikthrough is changing the way people around the globe interact with their computers, televisions, and mobile device screens. It has created a profitable, interactive model for the future of video where all the players—producers, advertisers, and consumers—get exactly what they seek from video-based interactions. Clikthrough's software enables constituents of the video value chain to measure and monetize its impact on the consumer market by individual video frame:
  - ▸ Video viewers can click on video elements to learn more about the product, person, or place, to answer such questions as: What brand is that power tool, and where it is available? That backpack is exactly what I've been looking for, where can I get it? Who is that new character on the show? I want to know more about him.
  - ▸ Vendors are able to measure the impact of product placement and their brand at the micro-level of exposure, per video frame.

Why Project Management Is Necessary for this Company

Project management tools and methodologies are used to orchestrate the work being done around the globe, eliminate the issues of time zone differences on effective communication, meet feature enhancement commitment schedules to customers, and ensure all software development activities are in line with the firm's core business strategy and objectives.

Executive Management Attitudes on Project Management Certifications

Regarding the organization's attitude toward project management certification, Abe McCallum stated, "At this point in the company's growth, we have not sought out certification in the people that we have hired. We look for the fact that they have a fair amount of project management experience and at the methodologies they have used in managing projects. We look to their skill sets and aim to hire talent. We are a small team. As we grow, we will probably have more rigorous checks and balances as far as certifications are concerned."

Project and Portfolio Management

Clikthrough uses project management to support the firm's overall business strategy, and to closely monitor the value-add toward successfully executing the larger strategy that each individual project contributes to achieving the vision. As a small firm, it is important to know what and how prospective projects contribute to the big picture goals and objectives.

Clikthrough must balance customer-requested features and functionality enhancements against its larger software vision. In McCallum's words, "There are a lot of moving parts, and so it has required us to build several different software pieces to come together as one to really provide the framework that our customers need."

When weighing one project against another, Clikthrough considers the following impacts:

- "With our business, two of the big driving factors are how to get to revenue and then how to get to profitability as quickly as possible to minimize the amount of capital we have to raise. Equity from investors is weighed more heavily than the revenue that we have, so we like to get as much revenue as possible."
- "It is very quick to see what the ROI is on a potential endeavor, especially if we are working with a very large company. We have to gauge, if we choose not to work with them today at this price, will we potentially miss out on future opportunities."
- "If we choose to take on work that may pay us less revenue, we are hindering our ability to complete software projects internally which could be of more value to us in the future. Internally developed software for the company's framework goals is a hard, tangible asset; it is our core intellectual property."

We need to determine:

- "How does deprioritizing an existing project potentially impact other projects underway, as well as impact the overall company strategy?"
- What are the costs to develop versus how the product will delight existing customers, fit within the overall company strategy, and create new revenue streams and market opportunities?"

Benefits of Using Project Management Tools and Methodologies

As a start-up in an emerging market, Clikthrough is singularly focused on achieving its core business objective of developing a framework that will meet its customers' and prospective customers' interactive video requirements. To achieve that vision, Clikthrough works on many software projects concurrently that must ultimately come together and interoperate as a single solution.

McCallum identified the following items as benefits gained from Clikthrough's use of project management:

- "The greatest strength is that it hold(s) you to a core set of requirements that you must adhere to."
- "It establishes a baseline framework of how everyone is going to communicate on a particular project, using the same terminology, set of documents, all providing the information that everybody is looking for."
- "Project management tools are helpful because most of the tools provide a way for you to have and retain discussion threads."
- "The tools provide document storage. They enable us to go back and say this is a project we worked on, what the people were talking about, and all the information associated with the project."
- "The interesting thing about project management is the ability to get the information exactly when you need it, as fast as possible, so you are not sifting through the organizational files and trying to find exactly what you need."

Defining Project Success

Clikthrough uses constraint metrics in measuring project success, but it also includes a few metrics unique to software development, and especially the interactive video market. McCallum noted his company defines project success based on:

- "The performance of the application."
- "How the application directly relates to the firm's framework vision."
- "How many bugs have been closed by the time we release the first version."
- "Upon release, how many bugs are being identified."
- "The turnaround time to fix those bugs, and our costs expended in that effort. The time it takes to fix something again and again directly relates to lost opportunity in new areas of development."

Establishing Work Breakdown Structures, Managing Expectations, and Improving Communication Flows

Clikthrough uses project management software in the cloud. This model provides everyone around the globe immediate access to project information including the WBS, issue logs, reports, and project status. In addition, cloud-based environments provide the storage needed for establishing historical project records and making the project histories readily available to all members of the team no matter where they reside geographically.

McCallum discussed how using project management tools in the cloud added value to the team and improved communication flows:

- "As a team, across all levels, we have an opportunity to see exactly where the project is and what needs to be done to get it completed."
- "It allows each person who has a role in the project to understand what the milestones are and what his or her direct contributions are to meeting those objectives."
- "Everybody can take ownership of the project because they all have a vested interest in getting it done on time."

How Project Management Helps Mitigate Pitfalls

In the software development environment in which Clikthrough operates, McCallum identified project pitfalls and mitigation strategies as coming down to managing many risks arising on the "customer side" through an emphasis on excellent communication with all the parties involved:

When the risk of the project failing occurs on the customer side, such as an executive leaving or withdrawing from the project, McCallum shared these experiences:

- "We utilize Clikthrough's internal management skills and relationships at that company to try to find out who is now going to be in charge of the project."
- "Communicating with the new lead as quickly as possible is crucial in our efforts to bring the project in on time, or to make him aware of the impact of changes on the delivery date."

Other risks associated with project delivery delays and pitfalls include financial impacts, market and brand reputation, and overall IT impacts. Financial impacts to a firm for failing or failed IT projects can be substantial, and include expenses associated with service delivery penalties, and costs associated with adding assets to get the project completed. Performing risk management throughout the project is critical to avoid these outcomes.

Finally, one failed IT project can have a ripple effect throughout all current and planned IT projects. IT initiatives are designed to be built on top of each other for improved business enablement. If an IT project fails, other IT initiatives could be in jeopardy.

Clikthrough's McCallum offers the following suggestions for mitigating risk:

- "A quality project manager will budget additional time for a new, unfamiliar project."
- "Pay attention to the project's performance metrics and milestones. Add resources where appropriate. A contractor at $15K now is substantially cheaper than the costs associated with a month's delay, lost opportunity costs, and brand reputation."

Post-Project

At Clikthrough, the post-project review is very important to the company's ongoing strategy. Each project undertaken addresses not only the customer's concerns, but adds to the intellectual property and framework of Clikthrough's overall corporate vision. Because each project is so critical to the company, the post-project activities are highly structured. McCallum said:

- "My team is required to build a PowerPoint presentation that analyzes the original scope of the project based on time, cost, and scope, and compare them against what was actually delivered."
- "We work toward identifying what were the wins and losses within each of the work packages. To be fair, what we look for is the opportunity to improve our people's skills. Because in each one of those scenarios, where something has fallen behind, or in an area where we were ahead, it was a direct contribution that is generally linked to one specific person."
- We like to recognize those people that were exceptional in the project."
- When you figure out how to manage your time, you become very good at realizing how to manage other people's time and that's what a great project manager does."
- "Most of us have a general gut idea of about what it takes. We'll put our finger in the air and say it will take this long, from a business sense, where the world changes every single day. That is not the right answer. Challenging people to really put a hard number on it, then hold them accountable to it, is a very important metric. I use accountability to evaluate who the team members are who are growing in the organization and where we need to look at making changes."

Words of Wisdom

McCallum had these nuggets of advice regarding project management for IT:

- "The best piece of advice I can offer anyone is to stay ahead of your team. You don't have to be the best at what they do, you just have to be thinking ahead of what they are doing and looking for problems in the project. You look to correct them before they come up."
- "After you have identified the project, try to find every possible thing you can do to draw out the information and get it down on paper. It will give you a very good idea of exactly what it is going to take to get it complete. Then factor in reserves to cover known and unknown risks."

- "I am extremely focused on project management. Even if we are not good at it, we focus on results. Project management gives everyone a very clear idea of who is accountable. As an executive, I am always accountable and everyone else needs to be as well. As a start-up, you can live or die every single day if you don't do things right. Bigger companies, such as Microsoft, can weather time because they have plenty of customers and they have lots of money in the bank, they can adjust (to project delays), and weather storms longer than we can."

Evolution Technology Group
www.ETG.net

The following is based on a personal interview with Mr. Jay Helms, vCIO at Evolution Technology Group (ETG).

Company Background

- Evolution Technology Group (ETG) is a medical industry outsourcing IT company.
- The company was founded in 1997.
- ETG is headquartered in Birmingham, Alabama, USA.
- It works primarily with private practice physicians in the southeast United States to install and manage the technology infrastructure that enables private doctors' offices to operate at extremely high rates of efficiency. The technology infrastructure is built to support software applications specific to the medical industry including practice management systems, electronic medical records, laboratory solutions, imaging systems, hospital integration, and insurance filings.

ETG provides its customers a choice between on-premise installations with monitoring and managed services, collocation, or a hosted solution at its data center. The intelligent application of technology enables ETG's customers to focus on practicing medicine, improve client satisfaction through faster, more accurate diagnostics, and expedite insurance filings. The private practices are also able to reduce excessive overhead expenses and human errors associated with paper-based records.

Why Project Management Is Necessary for this Company

ETG's prospects and customers cannot afford a single day of technology-related downtime. Technology touches everything in the doctors' offices from scheduling appointments to documenting laboratory results to processing insurance filings. Waiting for an IT outsourcer to obtain a piece of equipment or to get an application loaded is just not an option for the private practice medical business.

Project management tools enable ETG to track equipment orders, monitor rollout progress, stage and test the hardware and software at its facilities, and implement its solutions without any disruption to its customers' businesses. Every engineer on the ETG team has visibility into the cloud-based project management application. This allows each engineer to see his or her role and how it interplays with other engineering activities in the successful execution of each client's implementation.

Executive Management Attitudes on Project Management Certifications

ETG has been using project management tools and methodologies for the past several years. In Helms' words, "We were doing what we thought was ad hoc project management. After some of us obtained our PMP certification, our eyes were opened up; we were doing it completely wrong. It was very transformational for the team. The technology engineers have said, 'This is a total change in how we are doing things. It is so much better.' "

Today, recognizing the dramatic improvements in project rollouts, increased customer satisfaction, and reduced number of post-project trouble tickets, ETG management encourages its IT engineers to pursue the PMP certification.

Project and Portfolio Management

ETG uses project management to support the firm's overall business strategy of growth and continuous improvement of customer satisfaction measures. As a small, regional firm, it is important to know what and how prospective projects contribute to the firm's goals and objectives.

ETG must balance customer-requested timelines for implementation against its existing project schedule. For ETG, there are discrete phases that must be performed in sequence. Moving out of sequence has proven to be problematic for both ETG and the customer.

Projects are implemented on a first-in, first-out basis. A larger, more lucrative private practice implementation contract that gets signed after a smaller project is underway is queued up to get started as resources become available.

The company uses project management tools to assist in identifying when new contracts can be launched. Communicating launch dates to prospective customers early in the contract negotiation process, and meeting those agreed-upon dates, is part of the firm's emphasis on customer satisfaction.

Benefits of Using Project Management Tools and Methodologies

As a regional vendor focused on a specific vertical market, ETG is keenly focused on achieving its core business objective of customer satisfaction.
ETG has a highly structured roadmap for project implementations starting with a professional services engagement to identify what, if any, new hardware and/or software needs to be ordered to meet the customer's objectives. Helms noted several strengths of using project management tools, including:

- "We use project management tools to build our implementation templates and work breakdown structures. We are able to reuse parts of these documents in a substantial part of our engagements, and our project management tool supports our templates."
- "The WBS is used to assign accountability for each work package in the project. Having that information at our fingertips has allowed us to quickly figure out we were going to have a problem when an engineer was out on extended sick leave. We were able to address the problem before it became a problem."
- "The project management tool has been extremely valuable for tracking equipment orders. We don't stock anything in-house. We don't order anything until we receive a deposit check or a signed contract from a client. So that can be another real tight timeframe for us. We have to make sure the vendors have all of the equipment in stock. Sometimes there may be backordering on equipment, but we try to put a little contingency play in the plan just in case."

Defining Project Success

Jay Helms said:

- "Using project management tools has enabled ETG to substantially improve its customer relationships by focusing precisely on customer-defined expectations identified in the project requirements conversations."

Establishing Work Breakdown Structures, Managing Expectations, and Improving Communication Flows

ETG's project management tool is in the cloud, allowing the engineers to look at the workflows and next steps when it is convenient for them. Helms couldn't say enough about how the tools have helped to manage the team's expectations and vastly improved internal communications.

- "Prior to using project management, we would have a team of engineers that would just show up on site. Once they got on site they would say, "I'm going to do this and this." They did what they were good at, but some work wasn't being addressed. That really impacted our customer satisfaction. Now, there is a game plan ahead of time, before we actually start. No work gets dropped. The customers are happy."
- "The WBS definitely helps lower the frustration level of knowing who's supposed to do what. Making work assignments based on work packages in the WBS helps to manage the expectations. Having the WBS and the project management tool in place has enabled us to set their expectations a little better."

- Before I got involved and got my PMP certification, we never had a pre-deployment meeting where we sat down and talked about the client, here's what to expect, and when you get on site, here's who is doing what. We do the pre-deployment discovery phase and come back and sit down again as a group. Here is what we found, here is what we will be doing, and here is the deployment. We make sure everyone understands their assignments."

- "Using project management tools has also lowered the engineers' stress levels, that anxiety level everybody has when you're expected to do something, but you don't know what that something is. Now, everyone knows exactly what is expected of them and when in the process it is expected."

How Project Management Helps Mitigate Pitfalls

Understanding how to address challenges that arise in a project and developing scenarios that will mitigate them is a valuable asset for every project manager. At ETG, the turnover within the engineering team is extremely low. They have not had to face addressing a team member's departure in the middle of a project. However, Helms notes, they would be prepared to handle that problem since implementing project management procedures. Helms commented,

- "Our engineers are cross trained. Should one leave mid-project, we could pull somebody from another resource such as a different team or even the CTO himself. That's one of the advantages of having a specialized business strategy. Our projects are very similar from one to the next. If an engineer is not involved in the project from the very beginning, then if they have to be thrown into the middle of it, they aren't far behind."

- "From a client standpoint there have been occasions when the administrators, who we primarily deal with, will resign in the middle of a project. Those are a little bit trickier. If you look at a project where we are just implementing new hardware, we will get through that phase. But if there is an administrative change during the report, monitoring and management stage of the project, then that requires us to engage in more extensive relationship management communications."

- "Although the procurement process is designed to prevent such occurrences, should one vendor not have the equipment we need for a project when we need it, we have a database of multiple approved vendors, and can quickly obtain the equipment from another source.

Post-Project

ETG uses a portion of the tools and processes of project management. Part of that is due to the relatively recent introduction of project management tools, and part is due to the nature of the company. Being focused on a specific vertical market allows the company to develop a high level of expertise in the best technologies that support the industry-specific applications. The company has also developed a highly refined playbook of best practices specific to the medical industry.

At the completion of a project, the project managers meet to identify areas that were exceptionally well executed, to be able to incorporate those successful processes into the next project's plan. The project managers also identify areas that were troublesome and investigate the contributing factors in order to avoid similar problems on future projects.

The company conducts a formal handoff to its services team. They introduce the customer and discuss the level of monitoring and management that is expected over the next year. The emphasis is on customer service and satisfaction. As Helms repeatedly noted,

- "We are industry-focused. We only do private practice medical. Everybody knows everybody in this industry. As our president refers to it, 'We are in a fishbowl. Everybody knows what is going on everywhere around them.'"

ETG also takes advantage of its ability to store and archive the project-related documents, creating an archive of all its project files. Helms said:

- "Our project management application allows us to save each and every project as a template. Then you can just build off that template. That's part of what we do. We also have documentation on our network about statements of work, RFPs, and all the other customer project-related materials."

Words of Wisdom

Helms said:

- "I've found that within multi-shareholder clinics, the success of any IT project relies on the soft skills of the executive management staff, specifically communicating with all of the stakeholders in their preferred mode of communicating."
- "Project management has allowed us to focus on and improve our customer satisfaction. The tools have improved the pre- and post- project communications

between us and our clients. We have been able to correlate project management with CRM to improve customer touch, help build our brand, and improve our reputation in the medical industry."

- "I think the strength of project management is the coordination of resources and making sure everybody on the team understands what is going on. And the project manager understands how much time the team needs to accomplish certain tasks. It improves communications across the company and between our company and our customers."

- "Using project management methodologies, we are able to clearly see what the next steps are to grow our firm and our engineers. We see where our time is spent and when is the best time to incorporate lunch-and-learn meetings to keep our engineers up on emerging technologies."

- "Project management affords ETG a structured way to see into our company, identifying our strengths and areas we need to shore up."

The Procter & Gamble Company
www.pg.com

The following is based on a personal interview with Alice Ferone, Associate Director for Global Business Services (GBS), Global Operations at The Procter and Gamble Company (P&G).

Company Background
- The Procter and Gamble Company is a publically traded company.
- The company was founded in 1837.
- It is headquartered in Cincinnati, Ohio, USA.
- In 2008, the company had net sales in excess of US $83.5 billion.
- The company has approximately 138,000 employees spread across facilities on nearly every continent around the globe. It conducts business in more than 80 countries.
- The Global Business Services (GBS) organization consists of approximately 7,000 employees, of which approximately 4,000 are directly involved with the company's information technology team.

The company has grown from a small, family operated soap and candle company to a multinational organization with dozens of well known brands spanning numerous markets including beauty, grooming, health care, pets, fabric and home care, and baby and family care. P&G's growth stems from innovation as well as acquisitions.

Why Project Management is Necessary for this Company
Every business unit within P&G looks to GBS for technology innovation, business transformation, IT implementation, and support. GBS services ensure standardized business processes and tools across the company to enhance business efficiencies in and between every global business unit and market development organization. GBS is responsible for providing technology-based solutions at a low cost and with a minimal capital investment. Technology plays an important role in P&G's business strategy and ongoing process improvement objectives.

At P&G, many of the IT initiatives are programs; collections of incremental projects that make up a substantially larger output. Programs run from several months to several years. Project management methodologies ensure every stakeholder associated with a project is up to date on the status of the work, who is accountable for work package fulfillment, and how all of the different teams' efforts influence and impact every milestone along the path to completion. In addition, project management enables the program manager to see, at a glance, how the incremental projects are enabling the larger program outputs.

GBS uses numerous tools to engage in a rigorous process of project evaluation relative to business value, to determine project prioritization, and to establish stringent project management best practices and methodologies. Once an initiative has passed through the vetting process, additional tools are used to closely monitor and manage the initiative. P&G aims to use the best tool for the size and scope of the project at hand.

Executive Management Attitudes on Project Management Certifications

P&G's GBS is accountable for IT innovation, implementation, and support across the global organization. To maximize its execution efficiencies, the business unit leverages industry standard project management tools, best practices and methodologies, and develops internal best practices based on strategic project learnings. The executive-level attitude is aimed at professionalizing the P&G portfolio and project managers via certifications, training, tools, and methodologies.

Within the IT team, the firm seeks to hire based first on leadership skills then on project management skills, but strongly encourages and supports new and experienced employees to obtain project management certification. The company also has a budget for employees to attend courses and project management training programs, ensuring their skills are kept sharp and current. According to Ferone, "We want to build and maintain project management competency in our people and instill the rigor needed to drive exceptional business results."

Project and Portfolio Management

P&G and GBS's global capability-building project portfolios are managed using standard processes and tools. There are multiple steps in the project evaluation process. First, every project is vetted through a business-centric scoring process to ensure the initiative meets the company's or business unit's strategy. Then the projects are ranked using financial metrics including Net Present Value (NPV), NPV per cost, and NPV per FTE. After additional application of hard business metrics to the initiative, each project receives a cumulative score that aids in project prioritization, ensuring P&G selects the best programs to achieve its business goals.

Ferone stated, "Once the cumulative scoring is completed, we apply judgment based on the business strategy to produce our overall set of project priorities."

The project portfolio within GBS, on average, consists of about 1,000 to 1,500 projects at any one time. Nearly all of the projects are managed by a project manager, with most of them managed using project management tools. Depending on the scope of the projects, a project manager is responsible for one to five projects at any time.

Ferone noted that, "Top projects are led by a PMP or someone who is highly rated in P&G's internal PM competency. We have an internal assessment we use to assess individual project management competency. The assessment defines the project manager's skills as proficient, advanced, or master. This is another method the company uses to nurture and grow our project managers' skills."

Benefits of Using Project Management Tools and Methodologies

At P&G, project management tools and methodologies are critical to its ongoing success. The myriad of project management tools used enables the company to effectively and efficiently manage its smallest projects to its largest initiatives.

The more efficient P&G is in taking a project from concept to completion, the greater the overall benefits are to the company, including return on investment and opportunity costs. Ferone noted that using project management tools and methodologies provides P&G the opportunity to deliver projects with speed and excellence while growing its employees' skills and establishing robust practices for future implementations.

Ferone also commented that, "The strengths of using project management tools and methodologies are in the professionalism and rigor they provide the company. We grow mastery in our project managers and establish best practices and rigor that drives project successes. This leads to the Company greatly valuing and investing in future IT capability."

At P&G, projects range in size and scope from less than 30 days to several years. There isn't one tool capable of supporting this breadth of scope. The net result is that each project manager has to be fluent with several different tools. It is important that each PM use the correct tool for the project being managed.

Ferone also noted, "Sometimes steps are skipped that come back to bite us. The way that we try to mitigate that is through Project Quality Reviews (PQRs) and peer reviews to help less experienced PMs "see around the corners" and build quality in, and via gated reviews where we have clear success criteria and a sponsor/stakeholder accountable to sign off at each stage that we have a proposition that warrants investment and moving forward."

Defining Project Success

For P&G, the project success definitions fit within its rigorous project implementation methodology. Specifically, Ferone pointed out the company uses Quality of Delivery and Quality of Launch metrics. She defined these metrics as:

- "Quality of Delivery is measured during pre-launch or just after launch (for Quality.) It is an execution measure to determine how the project is delivering on time, on budget, on scope, and on quality. We collect QOD for both the original commitment (the baseline set at project commitment), and the most recently aligned with the project's sponsor and/or the project board (current approved baseline)."
- "Quality of Launch is measured post-launch on our commercial initiatives to determine how well the initiative met its in-market objectives. It relates to the success criteria aligned with the sponsor and is reviewed at each stage gate. The measures are Value in Dollars, Value in User Adoption, User Satisfaction, and Client Satisfaction."

Establishing Work Breakdown Structures, Managing Expectations, and Improving Communication Flows

Ferone used P&G's integration of the Gillette Company as a specific example of how project management methodologies and best practices supported the smooth integration of two global companies. She emphasized the value project management tools and methodologies provided for risk management and communication across geographies and up the management chain. Noted Ferone:

- "We knew Wall Street was watching. The integration was being led as a global project. It had to go flawlessly."
- "At the time, I had responsibility for the North American integration of all of our global business services, systems, etc. I had a project schedule that addressed each service line of the business such as employee services that dealt with payroll and benefits and all the people systems, or our financial services dealing with the financial systems and reporting, or our supply network that covered ordering, shipping, billing, and the distribution network. Many, many areas of the company had project schedules that were thousands of lines long."

Ferone had a team of about 30 people, made up of people from both companies who represented each of the areas that were impacted by the integration. They came together on a weekly basis and reviewed key milestones.

- "We established what interventions were needed for any milestones that had the potential to go off track so we would stay on schedule for our preapproved cutover date that fit into the larger global schedule."
- "We used monthly status reporting and regional and global dashboards to communicate which service lines, which countries, and which regions were not on track, and identified any issues where help was needed."
- "These meetings and status reports triggered reviews with senior leaders to talk about areas that were off track, and what actions or interventions were required to get those pieces of the project back on track."
- "The Gillette Company integration was the largest, most comprehensive undertaking as a company we have done. It taught us a lot because it touched almost every area of the operation. It is an excellent example where we leveraged existing tools and created many new ones that elevated both the knowledge of the organization (how it all works together/key interdependencies) and robust tools/schedules/techniques that were reapplied on successive initiatives and acquisitions (e.g., Globally Aligned Schedules, Readiness Assessments, Risk Assessments, Dashboards, Control Rooms, Hypercare, Project Closeouts/ Learnings, etc.)."

How Project Management Helps Mitigate Pitfalls

Project pitfalls are the risks associated with project implementations. Risks are inherent in every project and understanding how to mitigate them is an essential skill for project managers.

At P&G, Ferone notes that managing project risk comes down to effective project planning and communication with the appropriate constituents. She also noted the importance of iterative testing along the project implementation path as a way to mitigate project risks. In addition, Ferone suggests the following to reduce the chances something will go wrong:

- "The project manager must proactively, from the beginning of the project, identify a network of powerful stakeholders and seek higher level support for a project that crosses multiple functions and/or geographies. This allows continuity of support and minimizes the risk of a complete change of strategy should a key stakeholder or sponsor change roles."
- "Leverage the established communications plan to ensure full visibility of past agreements and needed actions to drive continuity in the stakeholder engagement process."

- "Quickly join up and onboard a new stakeholder from the moment the announcement is made, so that the project is top of mind. This ensures that the project team and leadership view of the project is known by the stakeholder early, versus having their first impressions based on others' input."

- "If a project is slipping, or has had late deliveries on milestones, one option is to replace the project manager. It is not an easy decision, but it is sometimes necessary to bring in the required project management strengths and experience to get the project back on track."

- "To succeed with complex projects, the project management team must combine subject matter expertise and project management excellence. Sometimes you can find this in one person, but more times it means you need to have a combination of business and IT project managers that work together."

- "We have a very detailed up-front testing guardsman role that we call the SCQV (Shakedown, Commissioning, Qualification, Verification) leader. They are responsible for creating the overall testing plan, test scenarios, and monitoring unit and system testing. They are also responsible for our user acceptance tests or business tests, and ensuring that each test case is fully signed off. We track our test cases for completion; we do not start up until we have 100 percent completion."

- "We conduct 'what could go wrong' assessments at the end of every stage/ milestone of highly visible projects. During the Gillette integration, this really uncovered lots of possible scenarios. We put mitigation plans in place for high probability/high impact risks so that they wouldn't happen, or at least if they did happen we would minimize the impact."

Post-Project

At Procter & Gamble, the lessons learned sessions are viewed as a professional growth opportunity for everyone involved in the project. Ferone said,

- "We recommend that project managers manage and report on project impact for three to six months after project implementation. We ask that the project managers don't just launch and leave, but that they launch and continue to monitor it to ensure that it is meeting the business needs."

- "Many of our initiatives become part of overall services. Once the project is stable, normally within three months of completion, it is turned over to the Service Manager and supported as part of the ongoing service."

- "We encourage all project managers to do a project closeout where they capture lessons learned. What worked? What did not work? What would you do differently?"

- "We also have project quality reviews that occur throughout the life of the project. These reviews happen at each project milestone and at the end of the project. The reviews are then shared with all of the project quality review coaches and within the organization. This helps build project manager learning, plans, and leads to overall skills improvement."

- "We also do debriefings after each project in some organizations. The sessions are not about blame, they are about learning. So if the mission or project didn't go exactly as planned, you take off your project hat and come into a room where there are no levels, no hierarchies, and just evaluate, for the sake of learning, what happened. In this way, if we do a similar project, the next time we know what to do differently."

- "We are very successful at stopping projects and not making people feel like they failed because of a stopped project. It can be a reason to celebrate that you haven't poured more money into something that wasn't going to be successful. With the project closeouts, debriefings, and quality reviews, we focus on the learnings and what to do/not do next time to ensure project success."

Words of Wisdom

After nearly three decades at P&G as a seasoned project manager and organization leader, Alice Ferone has a highly refined perspective on project management. She and her global team offer the following advice to those beginning their project management careers:

- "First, the company needs to have a strong central PMO for successful management of the IT project portfolio."

- "Second, clear prioritization, choices, well defined success criteria, and definitive stop decisions are required to deliver projects successfully."

- "Third, time for planning and resource allocation must be built in to avoid a sub-standard product in the rush to deliver."

- "Fourth, you can't worry enough. The biggest issues or failures come from underestimated and missed risks. You can never look too broadly or too deep for potential issues."

- "Find project managers with a good combination of business domain knowledge and strong project management skills."

- "Finally, staff project key roles with people who have directly related experience and can therefore see the issues coming around the corner. Keep injecting outside perspective into the project via audits and peer reviews so that the insular environment, which tends to develop in projects for all the right reasons, does not become a source of major blind spots."

 SunGard Higher Education
www.sungardhe.com

The following is based on a personal interview with Pamela Bissa, Northeastern Region Project Manager Director, and Kevin Goss, Senior Project Manager at SunGard Higher Education.

Company Background

- SunGard Corporate is a privately held Fortune 500 company.
- The company is based in Wayne, Pennsylvania, USA.
- It has over 20,000 employees in 30 countries.
- The company provides service and support to more than 25,000 customers in 70 countries.
- The company is comprised of four divisions: Availability Services, Financial Systems, Higher Education, and Public Sector, which provide IT infrastructure and services, software, and processing solutions. SunGard Corporate is widely recognized as a leading global software application provider.

This interview focused exclusively on the SunGard Higher Education division and its use and application of project management tools and methodologies.

- SunGard Higher Education has a global presence with over 2,700 employees supporting over 1,600 higher learning institutions. It offers universities and institutions of higher learning:
  - ► Strategic consulting and professional services to assist institutions in aligning their administration, faculty, processes, and technology with the overall strategy.
  - ► Software and services that create a unified digital campus to meet all of the needs of the institutions' constituents, including the surrounding community.
  - ► Technology management to support IT's on-going management, strategic direction, services, and support.

Why Project Management Is Necessary for this Company

At SunGard Higher Education, nearly every client contract is a program; a collection of incremental projects that make up a substantially larger output for building out digital-based institutions. Programs run from a few months to a few years.

Executive Management Attitudes on Project Management Certifications

The SunGard Higher Education business is built on a foundation of project management tools and methodologies. All of its client engagements are fulfilled using a project management best practices methodology. As a result, executive managers have identified substantial value in the use and application of project management tools, and seek to support their employees in obtaining and maintaining PMP certification and skill sets. According to Bissa:

- "The executive management team aggressively supports project management and sees the value of project management to deliver services to our clients."
- "They invest a large amount of funding to enhance the PM leadership organization and fund PMI certifications across the globe."
- "Executive management has supported the implementation of a cloud-based project management office to support project dashboards providing visibility into specific metrics around each client's deliveries."
- "The company invests in retraining our project managers on improved PM methodology."
- "SunGard Higher Education performs regularly scheduled health checks for each of our clients as part of our formal coaching-mentoring process."
- "We have full support of the executive leadership team around project management and have their support in ensuring project management is always a part of any product or solution that we deliver."

Project and Portfolio Management

SunGard Higher Education's project portfolio is managed using a first-in, first-served model. This strategy is typical for companies of all sizes that focus on a specific vertical market. They are able to utilize the customer queuing method of project portfolio management because they have previously established and baselined the ROI on each application, product, and service they offer within their specific marketplace.

The project portfolio averages over 500 concurrent projects around the globe. In addition, there are more than 800 small work order projects that are managed by the project management administration team. Bissa stated, "Approximately 20 percent of our projects require a dedicated project manager for the duration of the project. Of the remaining projects, each project manager on average manages three to four."

The number of projects managed is expected to more than double due to a corporate reorganization. SunGard Higher Education is bringing the IT Infrastructure and

Services organization under the project management office. This reorganization is another data point reflecting the executive leadership's positive perspective on the value project management methodologies bring to the firm.

The reorganization is seen as a positive, strategic move for the company. It will enable tighter controls on the number and types of projects in which the company engages, improve resource allocation and distribution across the projects, and afford better visibility regarding the company's progress in terms of achieving its strategic goals and objectives. Positive results of the reorganization are already being seen in the increased number of larger client engagements that require a dedicated project manager.

The project portfolio is managed based on the overall business strategy. Projects are prioritized relative to the output's contribution to the division's overall goals and objectives.

Benefits of Using Project Management Tools and Methodologies

At SunGard Higher Education, the suite of project management tools and methodologies is critical to its ongoing operations. The project management office has so effectively established its value to the larger organization that it is in the process of incorporating a former standalone division. The collection of project tools used enables the firm to effectively and efficiently manage all of its projects from its smallest engagements to its multi-year programs.

It should be noted that SunGard Higher Education has developed its own project management tool, Higher Ground^{SM}. One component of the tool is its client dashboard. The dashboard, a visual model of key components of each project, provides the project manager, the project manager leader, and the executive team a view into the status of each project. It allows rapid response to any issue or potential problem before the situation can impact a program, a project, or the client.

Goss identified several strengths of Higher Ground^{SM} and its dashboard including:

- "The dashboard is used to direct resources to where unhealthy projects need support."
- "The heat indices, the green, yellow, and red status metrics, are used constantly as a measuring device. We monitor the dashboards and provide immediate attention to projects that are potentially in trouble, by the red, yellow, green status."

- "Our project managers don't worry about missing milestones. The theme is 'don't worry—take action.' When used correctly, the tools and methodologies prevent worrying. You watch the tasks that lead up to the milestone and take action prior to the milestone slipping. Then you have nothing to worry about."

Bissa added:

- "The heat index has metrics around cost, scope, quality, risk, schedule, client relationship, and project-related issues. If there are no problems in any of those areas, the metrics on the dashboard are all color coded green. If there is a problem in an area, we mark it yellow. A yellow flag indicates there is a problem that we are mitigating."
- "A red flag indicates there is a problem that could be detrimental to the project."
- "There is a link in the dashboard that lists the risk or issue and the mitigation strategy."
- "Along with this dashboard, we perform project health checks on each project. Project health checks enabled us to be proactive when risk and issues arise."
- "The strength of project management tools and methodologies is providing a framework which the project manager can use to go manage the product or service that we are contracted to deliver."
- "We also use our project management tools to support our mentoring and coaching of project managers. We aim to have all of our project managers providing best-in-class project management services."
- "There is a perception that project management slows the process down and adds administration overhead to the project.
- "Frankly, that's the biggest reason why some companies don't support, and don't implement, a strong project management foundation. There is a perception that it slows down the implementations. What they don't understand is if you don't plan up-front, the action of not doing that groundwork will increase the length of the project in the long run."
- "Project management forces you to document each step. In the end the client appreciates the documentation. Today, we find that more and more clients understand the value of using project management methodologies."

Defining Project Success

For SunGard Higher Education, the customer relationship management and quality aspects are extremely important. Bissa emphatically noted the company defines project success as:

- "When our project meets the client's expectations, we have delivered the services and the products as the client expected that they would be delivered."
- "Meeting our client's expectations is what tells our executive team, our sales team, and our delivery organization that we were successful. We delivered exactly what the client expected out of the product or the service that they purchased."

Establishing Work Breakdown Structures, Managing Expectations, and Improving Communication Flows

SunGard Higher Education uses its internally developed Higher Ground[SM] project management tool, its dashboard and heat index measures, and Microsoft's SharePoint for collaboration and information sharing. This model enables everyone immediate access to project information including the project scope statement, project budget, WBS, risk and issue logs, and project status reports. In addition, the SharePoint site acts as storage for establishing historical project archives and making the project histories readily available to all members of the team no matter where they reside geographically.

The company relies heavily on project management methodology during initiation and planning to set expectations, establish the scope of services, develop the schedule, and define the detailed project budget. At the same time, it is important for the project manager to establish project rules of engagement with the client so that the proper communication flows are established immediately.

According to Goss:

- "We start with project governance documents early in the cycle–the project charter, scope statement, and project management plan. Those are our first deliverables or milestones. We do a project charter to start, we set the scope. This sets up a strategy for doing the WBS as we go forward."
- "We start with a WBS template, but we build into the template how we are going to massage the plan as we go forward. We reconfirm goals and objectives at the beginning of the project. Make sure we are all headed in the right direction, looking for the right accomplishments throughout the documents."

- "All that time and activity at the beginning of the project with the client is spent ensuring we get off to the right start with the project governance documents."
- "The scope document sets the expectations of what's included and what isn't in the project."
- "We also set up the tracking mechanism early. How are we going to track progress? Are we going to have monthly status reports or biweekly status reports?"
- "We define when we are going to have our weekly meetings. Part of the agenda items for those meetings is going to be a review of the tasks in the project plan. We set all of those expectations early. We follow the methodology, and then we don't have to debate anything as we progress through the project."

Bissa added:

- "Our project management plan is our plan for how we are going to implement. That means, for example, how we include in that plan our risk management strategy: how are we going to monitor and control risk? The communication plan: how are we going to communicate? How are we going to manage the scope?"
- "We talk a lot about our change management. We call it our Iterative Change Control process. That's where we lay the foundation of what changes will be monitored and how they will be viewed with the client."
- "Our project management plan gives the client confidence that we have the project under control. We are setting our rules of engagement and how we are going to work with each other."
- "We put a communication plan together that defines when the internal and client teams will meet to discuss project progress. The project manager then defines when the weekly meetings will be held with the client, who will participate, and whether the meetings will be virtual or on-site."
- "We then include a stakeholder review timeline. For example, the project sponsor from the client side might not want to be updated every week, but they may prefer an update every month."
- "We put our governance structure into the communication plan. We document when we are going to hold internal meetings. I am talking about documenting the detail down to the day it will happen, the hour it will happen, the conference line that will be used, if one is going to be used."
- "We document how often status reports will be completed, what template we will use for the reports, and what input is required from the project team in order for the project manager to complete the status reports."

- "We also have an escalation process that's outlined in the project management plan. It talks about who to escalate problems to, and when."

How Project Management Helps Mitigate Pitfalls

At SunGard Higher Education, Bissa notes that effective communication is critical to dealing with project risks. Specifically, Bissa suggests the following as a standard part of their risk response plan if, for instance, a key sponsor or stakeholder departs:

- "If a critical person on the client leadership side is no longer involved, we make sure the project manager gets access to the new person. We show them the project charter, review with them the project scope statement, and the baseline governance documents that were set up on the project."
- "We make sure that they understand the business value, the reason why we were hired to provide the products or services."
- "We give them the big picture, and then we drill down into the tactical picture of where we are by milestone. We share the current issues and risks that are on the table and what we are doing to mitigate them."
- "We make sure they are comfortable with the big picture, ensure it matches their expectations. It is possible the new guy could have been brought in to totally change the project. It wasn't moving in the correct direction that the executive leadership at that institution wanted it to run. So, the first thing we try to do is make sure we have baselined the project with the new person. And then, we drill down into the details to get them comfortable with what is happening today."

On a broader scale regarding change and change management Goss mentioned,

- "That is the value of the PM methodology, to closely manage the change control process. If there is a change, we will continue to work. Sponsors change, or whatever is going on, we will continue to work the tasks to meet the milestones, meet the schedule."
- "If someone has an issue, whether it is changing objectives or business strategy or whatever, we write up the issue, and examine viable alternatives. We make sure we do the impact analysis as part of the change control process; what is the impact on the project?"
- "We make sure all the stakeholders are aware of the impact of that change before we invoke or implement it. That really is a core piece of project management methodology; change control."

- "The project management methodology is figuring out what part of the WBS is broken. Project tracking will flush that out. You will start to see, through regular project tracking, where the problems are, whether tasks are going to be on track or if they are not getting completed. You have to dig in and see why they aren't getting completed. Which phase is it, which piece is it that's broken."
- "Frequently issues are around personnel management. That's a big part of what project managers do, manage people through the project."

Post-Project

Because of the iterative nature of its implementation model, SunGard Higher Education holds its lessons learned sessions after each module is in production at the client's site. The company also holds a final program lessons learned session.

At SunGard, the lessons learned sessions are an important part of bringing each module of a project to closure. Bissa noted the following value that comes from these sessions:

- "Typically our implementations are iterative. As we provide the suite of applications to the institution, each application implementation is its own project."
- "Oftentimes, once we have gone live with an application, we are already implementing the next release or the next module. It is an iterative approach."
- "We hold debriefing sessions internally and with the client."

Goss added:

- "We gather the different project teams with the client; we sit down with the team who worked on one module, for example, the finance people who worked on the finance portion of the project. We like to encourage people to talk about things that went well as well as things that didn't."
- "We aim to set a professional tone to the discussion. One person speaks at a time and addresses a single item. We go around the table. This way everyone has an opportunity to say something. We keep going around until all of the module's items have been addressed. It is the same process at the end of the program."

Words of Wisdom

As a seasoned, senior project manager at SunGard Higher Education, Kevin Goss has a field-proven perspective on project management. He offers the following advice to those beginning their project management careers:

- "It is important to communicate successes. Communicate them to the leadership team, to the project team, and to the client. For the project team, one way to do that is to have group breakfasts or group meetings after those milestones (are met) to communicate the success of the project."
- "Make a commitment! Commit to learning and applying the project management tools and methodology and also commit yourself to the success of the project. Projects are often successful due to the efforts of a small group of committed people. Be one of those people."
- As a senior project manager now in a leadership role, Pamela Bissa offers the following nuggets for beginning project managers:
- "Project management tools and methodologies are simply a framework. It is important to know you have the tools and how to use them. However, well-honed soft skills are what separate superb project managers from regular project managers. It is those soft skills: having the ability to lead; having the ability to communicate; having the ability to drive a team to one goal or one mission. Those soft skills are very, very difficult to teach."
- Soft skills can make or break the project, the relationship with the client, and the reputation of the company that you are representing. To obtain the soft skills, my advice is to hook up with a strong mentor or a coach or a senior project manager or somebody within the organization that is experienced and demonstrates strong soft skills. Doing project management successfully requires highly polished soft skills."
- "Effective communication is the key to success as a project manager. If you are just starting up as a project manager, I would highly recommend engaging with a mentor or coach that you trust and respect. Follow in their footsteps, follow in their path, and follow their advice to strengthen yourself as a project manager."

Index

A

Accelerated IT project timeline   18
Acceptance criteria   91, 109
Activities   101, 130, 131
Agenda   60
Art of project management   16
Assumptions   110

B

Benefits of a project charter   33
Benefits of a work breakdown structure   104-105
Business case   28
Business process improvement   20, 195

C

Change   14, 16, 19, 72, 89
Closing   14
Communications management   145-151
Communications management plan   152-153
Communications requirements   73, 147
Constraints   15
Contingency plan   164
Contingency reserve   168
Critical path   132
Customers   66

D

Deliverables   29, 99
Dependency   131
Duration   120, 131

E

Effort   120
End user   66
Estimating   110, 117-122
Evaluation   102

Executing   14
Executive management   187
Expectations   70-72

F
Failed/failing project   175-179
Fallback plan   164
Functional managers   66, 79
Funding sources   66

G
Ground rules   60

H
Historical information   55-60
Horizontal incrementalization   45
Hosted implementation   201
How to create a WBS   100-103

I
In-house implementation   201
In the cloud   201
Incrementalization   43-45
Initiating   13, 15
Interdependencies   110
Issue log   82-83
IT   1, 17
ITIL   196-197
Iteration   14,15

K
Kaizen   20

L
Lessons learned   60, 186
Level of influence   71

M
Management   65
Management reserve   168

Metrics   29
Milestone   110
Monitoring and controlling   14
Monte Carlo simulation   122-123

N
Network diagram   131

O
Open-ended questions   61
Opportunity   163-164

P
Padding   118
Planning   13-14, 19
Portfolio   48
Post-project   183-186
Product lifecycle   13
Product scope   87
Program   48
Project   43-45, 47-48
Project charter   27-30
Project life cycle   13
Project management   9
Project management office   66
Project management plan   15
Project management process   13-15
Project management software   130, 199-201
Project manager   66
Project objectives   29, 99
Project schedule   131
Project scope   87
Project scope statement   91-92
Public   66

Q
Qualitative risk analysis   165
Quantitative risk analysis   165

R

Recognition and rewards systems   80-81
Reports   147, 186
Requirements   29, 71
Research   102
Reserves   168
Resources   28
Risks   30, 163
Risk identification   165
Risk management   163-166
Risk management planning   165
Risk monitoring and control   165
Risk register   166-167
Risk response owner   165
Risk response planning   165
Rita's Process Chart   12, 194

S

SaaS   201
Schedule   131
Schedule management   139
Schedule model   131
Science of project management   11
Scope creep   37, 109
Shelfware   183
Six sigma   20, 195
Software as a service   201
Sponsor   65
Stakeholder   70-73
Stakeholder analysis   70-72
Stakeholder identification   65, 70
Stakeholder management   75-78, 83
Stakeholder requirements   29, 88-90
Stakeholders   28, 65, 83-84

T

Team   21, 66
Template   56
Threat   163
Three-point estimating   121-122

V

Value matrix   49-50
Vertical incrementalization   45

W

Watchlist   167
WBS dictionary   107-112
What-if analysis   134
Written communication   90
Work breakdown structure   99-106
Work package   101-102

FREE Online Edition

Your purchase of **PM Crash Course™ for IT Professionals: Real-World Project Management Tools and Techniques for IT Initiatives** includes access to a free online edition for 45 days through the Safari Books Online subscription service. Nearly every Cisco Press book is available online through Safari Books Online, along with more than 5,000 other technical books and videos from publishers such as Addison-Wesley Professional, Exam Cram, IBM Press, O'Reilly, Prentice Hall, Que and Sams.

SAFARI BOOKS ONLINE allows you to search for a specific answer, cut and paste code, download chapters, and stay current with emerging technologies.

Activate your FREE Online Edition at www.informit.com/safarifree

> **STEP 1:** Enter the coupon code: RZQXAZG.

> **STEP 2:** New Safari users, complete the brief registration form. Safari subscribers, just log in.

If you have difficulty registering on Safari or accessing the online edition, please e-mail customer-service@safaribooksonline.com